HOW TO FIND GOOD WORK **WITHOUT** A COLLEGE DEGREE

HOW TO FIND GOOD WORK **WITHOUT** A COLLEGE DEGREE

By Susan A. Lieberman

CONTENTS

A Note:

To keep this book from being too long, we have added lots of notes that will connect you to websites with more detailed information about subjects that interest you.

You will see the number of each note usually connecting you to a website with additional information at the bottom of the page as you read along. To make it easier for you to connect, go to the book's website where all these notes are listed in order by number:

http://susanlieberman.com/work/notes

If you open this page and keep an electronic gadget at hand while you are reading, you can go to any number that interests you and click through to the site noted. If you are listening to the audio version of this book, go to the book website and you will be able to access notes from there when it is convenient.

When we published this, all the links were working, but over time, some may not open for you. In that case, see if you can find the information elsewhere on the Internet.

For Cristal

Who cares so much and works so hard.

1

INTRODUCTION

The Work Proposition

Gotta work. Want to eat, have a place to live, go out for a pizza, see a movie, have a car? It all takes money. Few of us will be growing our own food and living off the grid. Most us won't inherit wealth or have anyone hand it to us. Stealing is not well advised. So we need work.

But work is more than money. Many of us take pride and satisfaction from being successful in our careers. If we value our work, whether it pays modestly or generously, it becomes a source of pleasure. If, as well, we find opportunities to keep learning and improving, satisfactions increase.

There is so much we cannot control. What we can control are the ways we see the world and how hard and smart we decide to work. What we want for ourselves influences what we get.

Negative emotions like fear, anger, worry and sadness affect memory, attention and reasoning. They make it harder to work successfully.[1] So among the skills that help us have successful careers are the skills of figuring out who we are and how to stay centered.

We have to know what we want. But remember, the people who hire us are also focused on what they want and need. They are looking to hire people who can help them with their goals. So there is the challenge: to find work that is good for us and that we can do in a way that makes us good for the people who employ us.

▶ If You Don't Like to Read

This book is meant to help you think about what you want with regard to work and how you might get it. If you **don't like to read**, listen to this book on audible.com. The audio reader can find numbered notes on the book website: http://susanlieberman.com/work/notes and connect to more information after listening.

---

1   https://blog.bufferapp.com/the-science-of-what-motivates-us-to-get-up-for-work-every-day

▶ How This Book Chose Careers

We looked for careers with these following qualities:

1. Careers that <u>offer a good chance over time of earning $20/hour or more once you master the basic skills needed and stick to it</u>. **If one is working full time, $20/hour is about $40,000/year. Yes, it may take time to work up to this income, but it is possible (NOT guaranteed) for the careers discussed here.**

   There are lots of good jobs that earn less than that. You, of course, can set a different number. This number was chosen with the help of a website from the Economic Policy Institute that lets you calculate a reasonable budget for a year. For more information about how we got to this amount, click on the note below.[2]

   You can find a geographic area on this site that interests you and type it in, fill in how many are in your family and it will tell you, on average, what it takes to fund a "modest yet adequate standard of living" for that area.

   The median hourly wage in 2016 (meaning half the hourly wages were more and half were less) was $17.86, which, based on 40 hours of work/week for 48 weeks is just over $34,000/year so we are aiming for incomes higher than the middle.

2. <u>**The job does not require a college degree. It may require specific kinds of training, but you don't have to go to a four-year college and graduate to land this job.**</u> **You do have to know the kinds of stuff the job requires, and education beyond high school will be required in the majority of cases. The most important skill you can develop for the 21ˢᵗ Century is the ability to learn how to learn. The world of work is changing very rapidly.**

   About 2/3 of people graduating from high school start a college program, yet only about 1/3 of the jobs in the future will need a college degree. According to the website noted below, two thirds of job openings in the coming years will be filled by people with a one-year certificate, a two-year degree or less.[3]

2   www.epi.org/resources/budget/ (I-1)
3   https://cew.georgetown.edu/wp-content/uploads/2014/11/Recovery2020.ES_.Web_.pdf

The more you know, the more skills you have and the better you will be able to do in the work world. There are many ways to develop skills, many ways to further your education. The trick is to pick the best ways for you. We want to help you figure that out in Chapter 5.

3. **We have looked for career options that are <u>not likely to be phased out by technology</u> in the next few decades. You have probably heard that many blue collar jobs have been lost in manufacturing, mining, retail, banking, etc. because technology has allowed companies to do more with fewer workers or because other countries are supplying goods that we used to provide in the U.S. The marketplace is now global. But if you are, say, a hairdresser, or a plumber, it's harder to be replaced by a computer or a person in China.**

The world keeps changing and there are no promises about what won't change. One prediction argues that humans soon will be unable to compete with the power of automation and data. Or it may be that what becomes most valued is upgraded thinking skills that allow us to do more than we yet think we can do.

We can't know how or when or where technology will alter the workplace, but we have looked for work that seems to have a fighting chance of sticking around for a while. And many employers are complaining that they have jobs but cannot find qualified applicants.

Some predict that the next few years will bring us as much change as the entire 20th Century. *If you take nothing else away from this book, take away this message: Learning how to learn will be your most valuable skill.*

▶ Gender

We know some jobs tend to appeal more to one gender than the other. We have not labeled any jobs male jobs or female jobs or any other gender variation, and we hope you won't either. Women can do jobs that were traditionally male jobs, like firefighter, and men can do jobs that have been labeled women's jobs like nursing. Look for what fits your personality and situation and baloney to the labels.

If you have a criminal record, you can still apply for a wide variety of jobs. Connect with this numbered note for more information.[4] And if you worry that employers may be concerned about your honesty, look at the Federal Bonding Program that offers six months of bonded insurance to employers. There is no cost to either employer or employee.[5]

▶ Is This Book Complete?

Lots of work went into trying to give you as much helpful information as possible. And yet, it's a sure thing that there are bits of advice, websites, ideas, etc. that didn't end up on these pages or information that will go out of date by the time you find this book.

So read this book, write in it, bend corners to take you back to pages that are important to you. But don't stop looking online, talking to people, finding other ideas. If you find mistakes or want to offer other suggestions, please use the website http://susanlieberman.com/comments to report them.

---

4   This is a list of hiring opportunities for people with felony convictions: www.trade-schools.net/articles/jobs-for-felons.asp and this is site with advice about how to discuss a prior conviction: www.careeronestop.org/ExOffender/FindAJob/GetInterviewReady/your-conviction.aspx
5   http://bonds4jobs.com/about-us

2

WORK BASICS

Behind this book is the hope that every person who reads it can do well in the work world. Our country needs you to be successful. Here are a few things you should know whatever career you choose.

▶ 1. Show up

Showing up is 80% of success but showing up includes showing up on time. Here's why: First off, it shows that you care, that you think the job is important and you want it. Second, it means your employers can rely on you. If you won't follow the show up on time rule, what other rules will you decide not to follow? And if you are not where you are supposed to be, it makes planning difficult. Third, it contributes to a fair workplace. If you get to come late, can everyone come late? Who gets to work what hours? Easier to have everyone work the scheduled hours. Maybe in time, more flexibility will be possible but not at the beginning.

▶ 2. Speak the truth

We all make mistakes. You are human. You will make mistakes. Don't lie about it. Don't blame it on someone else. Be responsible for your actions. This may, in some rare circumstances, cost you a job, but lying is even more likely to cost you the job; truth more often ends up earning you the respect of your employers and your co-workers.

When you tell the truth, don't be defensive, don't make excuses, don't get angry. Take responsibility and apologize. Just be a newscaster: This is what happened; this is how it happened.

▶ 3. Listen. Listen more

Don't be a know-it-all. It makes you sound phony and insecure. If you are not experienced, you will have a great deal to learn. Some people are good at giving direction and correction. Some people are bossy, demeaning, gruff, insensitive. Don't let those who communicate poorly get under your skin. Just figure out what you can do to make things work smoothly.

You just need to listen for content, for the information that will help you do the job better and develop more skills. Criticism can be uncomfortable, but if you can see it as a gift of information, you will do better. Here is a terrific talk about why it's so hard for us to hear criticism and how we can learn to hear it without stress.[6] And if it's unfair and no one is interested in your explanation, just move on. Focus on what's next.

Yes, some people do like putting others down. It makes them feel bigger even if, in truth, they are the smaller for it. So if you have a boss who corrects in a dumbass way, just take note of it so you don't make the same mistake when it's your turn.

▶ 4. Ask questions

Popular saying: There are no dumb questions. But yes, some questions are dumb, especially those that ask someone a question they just answered because you were not listening. But if you don't understand something, better to ask upfront. Or if you think something is wrong or unclear, ask. Asking questions and getting good answers is one of the best ways to learn. If you have a choice, ask the people who give the best answers.

▶ 5. Think like an owner – even if you are not

Owners care about their business. The best employees care as if they were owners. They make sure things are right; they pick up trash; they double check; they hold themselves to high standards; they want to get it done right; they think about how to do things better. Great workers are special because it turns out they are rare.

Now, here's a kicker. Sometimes you really are a great worker yet you are not rewarded. You are part of a big system that doesn't know how to distinguish and reward exceptional people. Or you work for a person who happens to be a pretty lousy boss. Sadly, it happens.

You may be stuck with this person for some time, and if you work for a lousy boss, you may want to find another job either in that company or another company. But

6   https://www.ted.com/talks/worklife_with_adam_grant_dear_billionaire_i_give_you_a_d_minus

be careful about pointing out to others just what a lousy boss yours is. Right as you may be, you risk being labeled as a complainer and you lose.

▶ 6. Stay Positive

Often people would rather work with someone who is likeable and kind than with someone who is not but is super-talented. It isn't any fun to have to spend all day with someone unpleasant or difficult. That doesn't mean, at all, that you should be a suck up, but it does mean that you should leave your troubles and problems at home and be agreeable to your co-workers. We are more likely to cut a bit of slack for people we like than those we don't.

It is also helpful to have good communication skills. When people talk to you, respond and do so with cheer and interest. The ability to communicate success-fully impacts most work situations.

▶ 7. No drugs

Many employers require drug tests as part of the hiring process and for continued employment. If drugs show up in your system, you will not be hired. A front page national news story in the summer of 2017[7] talked about two Ohio companies that needed workers for jobs paying $15 to $25 an hour, but as many as half the applicants failed the drug test. "We are talking to employers every day," says an executive with Northeast Indiana Works, a non-profit group that provides educa-tion and skills training, "and they tell us they are having more and more trouble finding people who can pass a drug test," he said. "I've heard kids say pot isn't a drug. It may not be, but pot will prevent you from getting a job." Just as alcohol is legal so may be marijuana, but you can't show up drunk and can't test positive for drugs which may impair judgment.

In addition to being able to pass a drug test, many employers require applicants to have an active driver's license so make sure you are in good standing with your state motor vehicle office. If you are male, you also need to register with Selective Service by age 26. See the note below.[8]

7   https://www.nytimes.com/2017/07/24/business/economy/drug-test-labor-hiring.html
8   is www.sss.gov

▶ 8. Learn how to do the job

You can show up on time, be likeable, have a great attitude and listen, but if you can't do the work, you are not very valuable. You have to learn how to do the basics . . . and then you have to learn more and keep learning until you are good enough to teach others. And still keep learning if there is more to learn.

Bosses are responsible for making a profit or keeping to the budget, for keeping clients or customers happy, for making good on what they have promised. They need employees who can help them do that. If you can't, you don't have value for the business. The better you can help a business meet its goals, the more valuable you are and the more you are worth to the company. So figure out what the goals are and how you can help.

▶ A Minute on Money

We started this book by noting that the need for money is what drives many of us to work. But you need to do more than get money. You need to know how to manage the money you get.

Growing your career and increasing your income is great, but it is even better if you learn how to manage your hard earned money. No matter how hard you work, how good you are at what you do, life can throw us unexpected curves. There may be a moment when the job you thought was forever suddenly vanishes or when you find yourself with unanticipated bills.

From the moment you start earning, start thinking about how you spend what you make and how you save some of that for a safety net and a retirement fund. Maybe when you just start out, that seems impossible, but even if you save just a few dollars a week, you are establishing a valuable habit.

There is enough to say about work in this book without taking on financial planning as well. So, first, find work you like and get started building a career. But while you are making that happen, start educating yourself about money.

You might want to look for free online financial planning classes. You can easily read, at no cost, all kinds of articles about everything from how to get the best credit card deal to how to buy insurance. This note sends you to an article with dozen of blogs about how to manage your money.[9] Or check out <u>wisebread.com</u> for articles on all kinds of ways to get good deals and manage frugally.

Two websites that seem to get high marks and are full of useful advice are DaveRamsey.com and NerdWallet.com. Ramsey is a good starting place if you are currently in debt.

Beware of friends or relatives who try to get you and your money involved in a can't-lose deal. If it sounds too good to be true, it is.

While this book aims to direct you to work that has the possibility of letting you earn $40,000/year, it may take time to get there and/or you may find your expenses are still greater. As you are marching towards your main career, think about whether you have a hobby or interest you can do on the side to earn a little extra. You might refinish and decorate used furniture, repair jewelry, make birdhouses, stencil walls, sew doll clothing, coach athletics, teach swimming, cater BBQs. There are so many niches that might not be sufficient for full-time work but are great secondary jobs and are fun for the people who do them. And sometimes, they grow into a full-blown career.

9   https://andthenwesaved.com/58-of-my-favorite-personal-finance-blogs-and-sites/

3

HOW TO FIGURE OUT WHAT'S RIGHT FOR YOU

A s your first step to finding the right career for you, start off by looking for clues, clues about you. The more you understand about yourself, the better decisions you will make.

On average, most of us spend about 60,000 hours working. We'll do it 30–40 hours every week, every year. It makes life lots easier if we like what we do, if we build a career – or several careers – rather than simply show up for a job.

A career is something that gives us a sense of accomplishment and keeps us learning and growing. A job is more likely to be something you do just for the paycheck.[10] Sometimes, we start out working a job and find we are developing a career. It can happen that one person considers what he does a career and another thinks it's just a job depending on how invested each is in the work.

Lots of career advice tells you to follow your passion, do what you love. Turns out, people who are clear about what they are going to love are the minority. And sometimes, what we say we love: shooting hoops, going to the beach, listening to music, skateboarding, etc. – might lead to a career but the odds are stacked against it. There are glorious stories about guys who started a garage band and it turned into the Rolling Stones, but few garage bands lead to stable employment. So how do you decide if you stick with something you love or keep loving it but look for a career elsewhere? Maybe there is a way to take what you love and use it to explore more work options than you first realized were there for you.

10 Not sure about the difference between a job and a career. Have a quick look here: https:// www.officevibe.com/blog/job-vs-career

TWO QUICK QUIZZES TO HELP YOU DECIDE WHICH CHOICES ARE BEST FOR YOU

1. Are you willing to do any kind of work you can find and live with very little money to keep doing this?

2. If you ask ten people who care about you but are neither your mother nor your girl/boyfriend, do they think you are really good at this?

3. Can you see yourself doing this when you are forty with a family?

4. Do you work hard to get better at this all the time?

5. Have you had any measure of success to suggest this could work in the future?

6. Does doing this make you feel good most of the time?

7. Can you do this without doing bad things to your body and/or mind?

8. Does doing this absorb most of your time and concentration?

There is no grade for this quiz but you need lots of YES answers to decide this will be your work. It's something you want to think about hard. Without those yes answers, it is probably time to consider other options. And maybe, even with them, you can figure out how to keep doing what you love while earning money at something you love less.

One more set of questions to help you move forward. If you can make yourself write down the answers, do it:

1. Do you seek out physical activity? Do you like to be outdoors and/or moving around?

2. Are you good with your hands? Do you like to fix things, whether they are hair or cars or appliances? Do you like to cook things, build things, make things?

3. Are you good with sports statistics or computers or figuring the odds on anything?

4. Are you a people person? Is it easy for you to talk with strangers? Do people like you and enjoy being with you and do like being with them?

5. Are you especially attracted to certain things or people? For example, have you always been comfortable with old people or animals? Have you collected something . . . rocks, butterflies, dress patterns. . .? What attracts your interest?

6. When you were a kid, what were your favorite things to do?

7. Do you know workingmen or women who have jobs that seem attractive to you?

8. What do you hate to do?

9. What would your parent, your best friend, your most critical teacher say you are good at?

10. What do you do when you have free time?

▶ Think About Your Clues

The answers to the questions above are clues, clues that offer the possibility of pointing you in the right work direction. Think of it like clues in a scavenger hunt . . . you have to take the information and decode it in a way that you can use. So, let's go back through each question with some comment on what to do with your answers:

1. **Do you seek out physical activity? Do you like to be outdoors and/or moving around?**

   If you disliked sitting still in school all day, if you get energy by moving and prefer being outdoors rather than inside, you want to look for work that won't pin you down to a desk or keep you in one place all the time.

   You may have done poorly in school because you hated sitting. This is NOT an indicator of how smart you are or how well you can do in the work world. Some of the most successful entrepreneurs were poor students.

2. **Are you good with your hands? Do you like to fix things, whether they are hair or cars or appliances? Do you like to cook things, build things, make things?**

   I have a Ph.D. My husband has a Ph.D. and an M.D. degree as well. We once spent an entire day trying to put together a Home Depot vanity for the plumber to install. We couldn't do it. The plumber came the next morning, kind of laughed at us and had it done in about 20 minutes. "But I have never read a book all the way through," he told us inept but book-busy academics. If you are one of those people I so admire who can do things with your hands and like doing it, to look for work that allows you to use this aptitude. We don't all have it. We have different gifts, and the world needs all of them. Find careers that need your mechanical aptitudes.

3. **Are you good with sports statistics or computers or figuring the odds on anything?**

   If you have a gift for numbers, there is a need for people who like math and can manage data. Maybe you didn't pay attention in math class but you can calculate sports statistics easily, figure out how to lay out a building project without much effort and/or play cards like a shark. Hang on to that information if it applies. There are many jobs looking for numbers skills, and you want to let interviewers know you have this ability.

4. **Are you a people person? Is it easy for you to talk with strangers? Do people like you and enjoy being with you, and do you like being with them?**

In many jobs, the better you are with customers, the more you will be rewarded. On the other hand, if you really don't enjoy talking with others and dislike people chatting you up, we don't want to send you in a direction that would ask for lots of interaction with people all day. You can say, "No, I'm not a people person," and still manage to talk with customers or clients but you might not want a career in which it was a significant part of the work. For example, cooks can cook without much chatter but waiters and waitresses get better tips if they are friendly as well as efficient.

5. **Are you especially attracted to certain things or people?**

Start with what you like and then look in a circle around that. For example, you say you have always liked the elderly. Does that suggest that you like helping people in general or that you especially are drawn to older folks? If you like rocks, is it because you have a general attraction to nature or science or things you can throw? Keep asking yourself: What is it about this that attracts me? Where can that attraction connect with a career?

6. **When you were a kid, what were your favorite things to do?**

What we enjoyed in childhood helps us think about what we might do as adults. If you were always taking things apart and putting them back together or sewing doll dresses or doing friends hair or building an engine, that's important data to use in your decision making about work. Remember, we often don't appreciate that we have skills that may be above average.

7. **Do you know working men or women who have careers that seem attractive to you?**

Having role models, people who can talk with you about specific careers and can help you plot a way forward and make contacts is a bonus. Even if you don't know people personally, is there something that has always been appealing to you? Look for categories easier to enter without exceptional talents unless you really do have exceptional talent. An interest can take you in many directions. Don't hesitate to explore all your options.

8. What do you hate to do?

Mostly, we are looking for ideas of things to include, but it makes sense to also think about what to exclude. Let's get anything you know you really don't like on the table. But here is a caution. Sometimes, we think we really dislike something because a parent did it or told us we should do it. Separate out people you don't like from activities you don't like, things you might do well from things you decide you won't ever do because somebody else thought you would be good at it and told you so. You can't choose your life's work based on somebody else's beliefs, but our family and friends do know us and sometimes their advice is useful. That should be one piece of our puzzle.

My long-time painter's son swore he hated painting and would never be a painter. Twenty years later, he is running his own small painting company, happily following in the footsteps of his dad who has taught him many skills and tricks to being successful. It just took a while to work through that original story about "never" without thinking about why "never" did or did not make sense.

On the other hand, don't let money be your overriding guide. You have to decide if careers that are dangerous physically or emotionally make sense for you beyond the money.

9. What would your parent, your best friend, your most critical teacher say you are good at?

Sometimes, others can see things in us that we miss. It's easy to assume that something we do well is not that hard and anyone can do it too, when, in fact, we have a talent. If a parent or a friend thinks you would be great at something in which you have little interest, it might not be a good idea at all. But listen to what others see your gifts and think about how you can use them.

10. What do you do when you have free time?

If you can link what you choose for pleasure with what you choose for work, you increase the odds of finding a satisfying career. For example, for every person standing in the center of a stage or arena, there are dozens of others that help make the performance or game possible. If you can't be the actor, you might be the set designer.

Okay, this information is now a filter for you. Take what you have written or just thought about and talk it over with people who know you well. See if they might help you get more ideas for where to look for work. When you look at some of the careers discussed here, put them up against your answers to see if they fit with how you describe yourself.

▶ And More Clues Still

In addition to these informal explorations, there are some well-developed tools that give you more information about yourself and where you stand compared to others.

Here's the thing:

- We tend to dismiss what we do well and give more importance to what we do poorly.
- We don't have very good ways of appreciating where we are better than average. I have been very successful in my work life because I have been lucky to find jobs that required the things I do well. But I am not so good at many more things than those I am good at. I am not gifted in math or pattern recognition or sound discrimination. I can't put together a big wheel without help, and I think if I went to hell it would mean I would have to spend mornings sewing and afternoons at Home Depot. Fortunately, my people skills, my aptitude for writing and research, my communication gifts, my ability to look into the future helped me build a good career.
- It's useful to identify what you are better at than average and find work that uses those skills rather than focusing on work that demands the things that are harder for you than others.
- We can learn to do things that don't come easily, but our odds of being successful increase when we build on strengths. And we each have personality

traits that make some work more pleasurable for us than other choices. The more you understand who you are, the more tools you have to use in making career decisions.

To figure out what you are better at than others, you can start with a free and quick online test.[11] And look at this web site suggesting ten free tests that help you figure out you.[12]

There is an excellent aptitude test, the Johnson O Connor Aptitude Assessment, that is very accurate in helping you understand how good you are at various skills compared to others around the country. But this assessment costs $710 and is offered in only 11 cities so try the free assessments first.

▶ How Do You Learn Best?

Too often, young people tell me, "Hey, I'm not very smart," as if smart were something fixed like height or eye color – something you had or didn't have. In fact, smart is more like ice cream – it is widely available and comes in lots of flavors, and you might have one flavor and not another.

A Harvard professor, Howard Gardener, spent his life studying and writing about how people learn and concluded that there are different kinds of intelligence. He describes seven kinds of intelligence or ways of knowing. Thinking about these might help you decide in what areas you will most easily find success:

1. *Linguistic intelligence*. You like words, whether talking or reading. You learn best with the traditional methods used in school – reading or hearing concepts explained to you – and it is a good bet you do well in school. You are talkative, you learned to read early and you don't mind putting your thoughts down on paper.

2. *Logical-mathematical intelligence*. You are interested in "how?" questions. You like to analyze situations and find patterns and rules that make things work. People with logical-mathematical intelligence are good with numbers, like calculating things and want to know why things work the way they do. You

11   www.whatcareerisrightforme.com/career-aptitude-test.php
12   https://www.monster.com/career-advice/article/best-free-career-assessment-tools

may like strategy games like checkers or chess and prefer to read instruction manuals rather than novels.

3. **Spatial intelligence**. It is easy for you to think in pictures, and you like to understand things by experiencing them either in fact or in your mind's eye. You may like to draw or paint or doodle. You probably enjoyed building blocks as a kid and now enjoy taking things apart or inventing things. When you describe things, you often use visual terms.

4. **Musical intelligence**. You hear more than other people. You easily pick up rhythms and interesting sound patterns. You have an ear for pitch and melody. You may make music or just like to listen and talk about it. Sometimes you miss the messages people are trying to deliver with words because you are distracted by the sound of the words.

5. **Bodily-kinesthetic intelligence**. Sitting all day in school is hard for you. You want – you *need* – to move. Maybe you are good in athletics or maybe you express your ability by working with your hands on artistic or mechanical projects. The more your body is engaged in learning, the better you learn.

6. **Interpersonal intelligence**. You shine when you are part of a group. You pick up accurately the feelings of others and understand their moods and motivations. You can use this gift in different ways. You may be the ringleader, egging others on to action, or you might be leading a street gang, or you might be president of the student council. It's the same talent.

7. **Intrapersonal intelligence**. Unlike the person with interpersonal intelligence, you prefer to work independently. You have a strong sense of self, and you are quite happy coming up with your own ideas and working on them. Others don't need to tell you what to do because you are busy figuring things out to do on your own.

Linguistic intelligence is most favored by traditional school programs, but once you know something about your preferred flavor of intelligence, you can use the information to figure out how to help yourself learn the skills you need for the work that attracts you.

If you have kinesthetic intelligence, you might want to dance yourself into learning. Put on a tape, grab your study sheet, shout out the information and dance it into your body. If you have strong spatial skills, you might want to put information into picture form. Use what works for you. Don't get caught in the "I can't" trap but focus on "How can I . . .?

But here is something you should know about these learning preferences. Recent research tells us that when people were given information directed to what they believed is their preferred style, they didn't learn the task any faster than if they were directed to use what was judged the best strategy for a particular task. So don't use your preferred way of learning as an excuse for saying, "I can't." As psychology professor Daniel T. Willingham tells us, "Any type of learning is open to any of us." Think about what you like as a way of understanding your preferences, but learn what you need to learn using whatever it takes to gain mastery.

▶ What Kind Of Work Is Most Likely To Make You Happy?

If the Johnson O'Connor tells us what kinds of skills we have naturally, another instrument, the Myers Briggs Type and Temperament Inventory (MBTI), tells us what personality preferences we were born with and how they show up in the world. When we work with our preferences and not against them, we are usually more content.

This website describes the sixteen different personality types according to the MBTI.[13] See which one you think fits you best. Then take a free online inventory to find out your likely type.[14] Use that information to figure out what kinds of work are best suited to your special personality type.

For example, one of the four scales that go into producing the sixteen personality types is extroversion verses introversion. Extroverts talk to think. Introverts think to talk. People who are stronger on the introversion scale may prefer work that does not require constant socialization or quick decision-making, but extroverts are going to want some degree of interaction to feel satisfied. Introverts can be very effective in talking with people but, unlike extroverts, they get their energy from solitary activities.

13   www.myersbriggs.org/my-mbti-personality-type/mbti-basics/the-16-mbti-types.htm
14   http://artofthinkingsmart.com/what-is-your-personality-type/

While free online tests without personal interpretation can be less accurate than working with an expert, this gets you started. You can always learn more about type by reading Internet articles or books.

The better understanding you have of your inborn gifts and your personality preferences, the more you can look for work that is likely to make you satisfied. Understanding different types will help you not only understand yourself but your co-workers and bosses and maybe even your family members.

4

....

JOB CATEGORIES AND JOBS

Conversation About 14 Job Categories

T here are different ways to get a fix on choosing your work. Suppose you want to take a trip. You could get a map of the U.S. (or even the world) that has every city, no matter the size, in every state and start thinking about where to go.

The way to do that for work is to begin with the *Occupational Outlook Handbook* that the U.S. government publishes. It lists thousands of jobs from A to Z.[15] Open it up on your device. Start down the list. When you find a job title that interests you, click on it. You will find:

- The median pay
- Kind of entry level education needed
- If there is an on-the-job training option
- How many jobs there are with this title
- How many jobs in this area are anticipated in the coming years

But when we think about going on a vacation, most of us don't start with the whole country. We pick a smaller area, maybe a state or region or a specific city. Or we might focus on an activity we like. So rather than look through thousands of jobs, start with a category of jobs or even one specific career path. We have picked fourteen broad job categories to consider that have opportunities that meet our career specifications.

1. The Trades
2. Community Safety
3. Water and Air
4. Entertainment
5. Hospitality
6. Health Care
7. Business
8. Manufacturing
9. Sales and Retail
10. Information Technology
11. Transportation and Logistics
12. Energy
13. Artisan/Artist
14. Entrepreneurship and Freelance Work

15   www.bls.gov/ooh/a-z-index.htm

Make use of the numbered notes in each category to learn more about it. And check out this note with even more detailed categories to explore.[16]

Every category has entry-level jobs that require minimal skills. It is always possible to begin at the bottom and work your way up, step by step, and sometimes, this is just the right way to begin. But often we direct your attention to apprenticeship programs in skill areas or certification programs that allow you to begin at a higher level with a better salary and more job security. That said, if you need to go to work right now and you don't have skills, yes, start anywhere but develop a plan for how you are going to move up.

As an introduction to looking for work, click on the note below for a good article on how to use the Internet to research job options and how to apply for a job, including how to write a good resume.[17] Another useful site that helps you understand the job application process is noted here.[18] Good information makes us smarter.

If you think you can benefit from one-on-one conversation about choosing work, try checking out the resources listed on the Department of Labor's CareerOneStop website.[19] Look for the American Job Center nearest you and all the other information links on this site. Make an appointment with a Center counselor. Some job centers will be very helpful. Others may disappoint you, but this is part of the hunting-everywhere-for-helpful-advice process this book advises.

As you go through the following pages, you may not want to read every category. But before you skip a section, think about whether there just might be something there for you.

16   https://www.thebalance.com/different-types-of-jobs-a-z-list-2059643
17   www.myperfectresume.com/how-to/career-resources/jobsrch/
18   https://www.thebalance.com/how-to-get-a-new-job-fast-2060712
19   www.careeronestop.org

1. THE TRADES

A computer is not yet going to come fix your leaky sink, misbehaving air conditioner or short in your electrical system. That's going to take a skilled technician. Take a look on the site in the note below for a good discussion of work in the trades and for a graphic showing the expected demand for plumbers, heating and AC mechanics and electricians.[20]

The next note will take you to a long list of all the work associated with the trades.[21]

Much of the work in the trades happens in the construction industry. According to the Bureau of Labor Statistics, (2014 data) there were more than 1.1 million construction workers tackling an exhaustive list of jobs. Many people enter construction as jack-of-all-trades laborers who assist tradespeople, but its possible to grow into a skilled worker whose talents are in demand. The average age of construction workers today is somewhere in the fifties. As they retire, the industry will need to replace them; machines cannot do all of this work.

Two options for jumpstarting a career in the trades are to get accepted into an apprenticeship program or earn a certificate from a community college or trade school. On the website in the note below, you can see the kinds of jobs in demand."[22] We are using this site because the information is good, but it only directs you to private trade schools about which we are cautious. Look for community colleges and apprenticeship training as well. Read the chapter that follows on Where to Get Skills.

One note about being part of a construction project. The work can be difficult. You can be working high above the ground or many levels below it, in the deep cold or unrelenting heat. There can be an element of danger although employers are obligated to provide safety measures, and you will be required to take safety classes. Think about whether this is something with which you can be comfortable. Increasingly, there is opportunity for women, but harassment, sadly, remains a reality on some work sites.

Here is a description of the work from someone with twenty years of experience.[23]

---

20   https://www.trade-schools.net/articles/trade-school-jobs.asp
21   https://www.theworkingcentre.org/types-trades/393
22   www.trade-schools.net/articles/trade-school-jobs.asp
23   www.streetdirectory.com/travel_guide/190856/careers_and_job_hunting/being_a_construction worker the good the bad and the ugly.html

2. COMMUNITY SAFETY

Computers can help police officers and firefighters but they are not likely to replace them.

If you are interested in becoming a police officer, go to the site noted below which will tell you the requirements and also how many police slots are likely to open up in each state in the coming year.[24] Police salaries may begin below our income level but fifty percent of officers, on average, earn over $40,000. With overtime, officers can reach six figures.

Police departments around the country have different requirements. Some want a two-year community college degree or even a B.A.; others ask only for a high school diploma or a certain number of college credits. Usually you will need to graduate from police academy training as well. Sheriffs and state troopers also do police work. Sheriffs are usually elected to their positions.

This note connects you to a good summary of the pros and cons of police work with links to many other useful related sites.[25]

Fire departments around the country, like police departments, have different requirements and salary levels. The process for hiring can be lengthy and will require both a written and physical skills test. Look at the note below for information about what is required in each state and how many job openings are anticipated.[26] And check out this helpful piece about becoming a firefighter.[27]

One doorway to the community safety field is as a security officer. These jobs generally pay in the twenties, but they allow you to gain experience and establish a work record in the field. A national listing of such jobs can be found here.[28] You might also explore work as a correctional officer.[29]

Another career related to community safety is the military. See the section on the military on page 77.

24   https://www.learnhowtobecome.org/police-officer/
25   https://www.thebalance.com/becoming-a-police-officer-974896
26   https://www.learnhowtobecome.org/firefighter/
27   https://www.publicsafetyelite.com/firefighter/how-to-become-a-firefighter/
28   https://www.zippia.com/unarmed-security-officer-jobs/
29   https://www.correctionalofficeredu.org/training/

Another area of opportunity is to work for the U.S. government as a border patrol agent or customs officer. You will need to take and pass an entrance exam and a fitness test in order to be considered for these jobs. Learn more here.[30] It can take a long waiting period to move up the list if you qualify, but in half a dozen interviews, job satisfaction seems high, and the salaries increase over time.

30   https://www.cbp.gov/careers/frontline-careers/cbpo

3. WATER AND AIR

With an increasing interest in climate change and environmental safety, there are now many careers related to water and air quality which are detailed in the note below.[31]

Environmental science and protection technicians typically need an associate's degree in environmental science, environmental health, or public health, or a related degree. Because of the wide range of tasks, environments, and industries in which these technicians work, there are, however, jobs that do not require any postsecondary education and others that require a bachelor's degree or more. Pay is influenced by education.

A background in natural sciences is important for environmental science and protection technicians. Students should take courses in chemistry, biology, geology, and physics. Coursework in math, statistics, and computer science also is useful because technicians routinely do data analysis and modeling.

Many technical and community colleges offer programs in environmental studies or a related technology, such as remote sensing or geographic information systems (GISs). While in college, students should include coursework that provides laboratory experience. Associate's degree programs at community colleges often are designed to allow students to easily transfer to bachelor's degree programs at public colleges and universities.

Jobs testing air and water quality may decline because of automation, but our increased interest in pollution and the effects of climate change could have a positive impact on the field. The outlook for careers here is still in flux. Some jobs will allow you to grow with on-the-job training through a series of step-up exams. Salaries will be low at entry, but there is opportunity to work towards more skilled positions.

31   http://www.pollutionissues.com/Br-Co/Careers-in-Environmental-Protection.html

4. ENTERTAINMENT

Okay, so you can't be Jennifer Lawrence or Justin Bieber. But behind every star performer are dozens of people contributing to the performance.

There are camera people, writers, set designers, costume designers, make up artists, agents, box office managers and producers. There are backup musicians and dancers, gaffers and location scouts. If you want to be part of this world, your best chances are to find a way in and work up from the inside.[32]

Think of all the places we look for entertainment: theaters, concert spaces, casinos, television, radio, nightclubs, bars, festivals, sporting events. Add cruises to the mix.[33] All of these have employment opportunities.

Many jobs in this category may be low paying to begin, but if you bring skills and talents, there are serious career opportunities. For example, the mean salary of makeup artists easily meets our criterion. With unions such as the International Alliance of Theatrical Stage Employees, the average gaffer makes between $30,000 and $70,000 per year, and electricians on big-budget films can make much more.

New York, Los Angeles and Las Vegas and other big cities are hubs for entertainment jobs. In other locales, you will have to be more imaginative. For example, cameramen and women work all over the country. They usually have at least an associate's degree in videography or journalism, but with talent and persistence, you might be able to demonstrate your ability to do the job. A niche site for jobs in entertainment is here in this note.[34]

Print and social media[35] have a role in entertainment as well. We read blogs, books, comic books, and magazines for entertainment, and we play video games and watch youtube videos avidly. Behind all of this are working people making it happen for us.

Although sports engages a huge portion of the country, and athletes require talent more than credentials, most of the sports-related career opportunities other than being the athlete favor those with college degrees.

32   https://www.thebalance.com/get-entry-level-entertainment-job-1283514
33   https://www.cruisecritic.com/articles.cfm?ID=1059
34   https://www.workinentertainment.com/
35   https://www.thebalance.com/social-media-skills-2063726

5. HOSPITALITY

Hospitality is a career category that offers opportunity any-where you live. It's a sector with easy entry and low wages at the bottom, but it is also a career choice with many opportunities.

Working at McDonalds may pay minimum wage, but an experienced waiter in a high-end restaurant, can hit the $40,000 income level with salary and tips and go far beyond. A beginning bellman might have trouble earning $20,000 a year, but the head doorman at a luxury hotel who is good at taking care of customers can earn $80,000/year. A hotel manager's median salary is in the $90s or up. See the note below for list of job opportunities.[36]

What does it take to do well? Showing guests and customers warmth, kindness, helpfulness and courtesy are important for success, and it can be a challenge because all guests are not courteous or kind in return. People who are success-ful here are good at solving problems and interacting with people. Developing the ability to mange others is a great asset, and this is a skill that can be learned. See the articles noted below for comments on the pros and cons of working in this industry.[37] [38]

A quick look at a Houston recruiting site had many jobs for restaurant manag-ers, all offering wages above $40,000 with benefits. You will have to work your way up to the management level, but if you are determined and focused and like working with people, there are lots of opportunities. The manager of one popular Houston restaurant says starting waiters, who are only hired for full time slots, can expect to hit $40,000 quickly plus benefits. Waiters who have been there many years and have long-time customers can go over six figures. "It isn't hard to teach someone how to serve food or place a drink. We do that all the time," this manager says. "What we look for is not experience but personality."

I sat next to a young woman at a concert who worked for fifteen years as a bartender. "This was great work for someone without a degree. I worked three nights a week, long hard nights, but I pulled in about $80,000/year." You have to be able to

36   https://www.thebalance.com/hospitality-industry-skills-2062407
37   https://www.soegjobs.com/2017/11/05/pros-cons-working-hospitality-industry/
38   https://www.monster.com/career-advice/article/break-into-hospitality

multi-task, schmooze and not get irritated by people who can be irritating. "There are always bartending jobs around," she says. "Just hang out at a bar you like, get to know the bartenders and let them know you want to work."

So far, we have talked about working in the front of the house, directly with customers. But there are lots of options in the back of the house as well. Harry's parents were unnerved when he refused to go to college and insisted on taking a dishwasher job at one of the best restaurants in Charlottesville. He knew he wanted to be a chef and thought the best way to learn was to work his way up. They are now, seven years later, quite proud that he is the restaurant chef. In my hometown of Houston, the owner of five well reviewed restaurants started washing dishing. Listen to his video.[39]

If you don't want to work directly with the public, you can book tours, bake bread, or work towards managing the maintenance staff among other options.

If, however, you worry about your good control around alcohol or drugs, consider another career sector. Especially in the restaurant business, access to these is often easy and enticing.

---

39   https://www.eater.com/2017/12/14/16776488/hugos-houston-hugo-ortega-video

6. HEALTH CARE

Health care has been a growth industry with many high paying career opportunities, but most well paying health care jobs require some degree or certification.

If you want a job that starts in the $40s, you are usually going to need to be certified in the specific area in which you want to work. This likely means a two-year certificate and often, you must have pre-requisite classes with good grades before you can apply. In some instances, there are apprenticeship programs that allow you to earn and learn at the same time.

Jobs in demand that meet our income criteria include:

- Cardiovascular Technician
- MRI Technician
- Licensed Practical Nurse
- Physical Therapy Assistant
- Clinical Lab Technician and Technologist
- Radiologic Technician

- Dental Hygienist
- Occupational Therapy Aid
- Registered Nurse
- Respiratory Therapist
- Surgical Technologist
- Massage Therapist
- Ultrasound Technician

Type each career title into your browser to find out the work each of these involves and how you prepare to enter the field.

There are other opportunities that take less time to prepare but the starting salary is less. Certification as a medical assistant can be earned in eight months and costs about $1,000. There are increasing opportunities for apprenticeships for medical assistants as well.[40] Salaries begin in the thirties, but this is one of the quickest ways to enter the healthcare field. The article noted below gives you details on the various options.[41] Once working, you can continue to develop your skills if you wish.

40   https://www.mynextmove.org/profile/apprenticeship/31-9092.00
41   https://www.medicalassistantschools.com/articles/cost-to-become-a-medical-assistant/

7. BUSINESS

This is a huge catchall category that can include the local tackle shop or a million dollar corporation. Businesses need all kinds of skills from number crunchers to customer service representatives.

Name a business and you will find a variety of career opportunities from across categories. For example, consider real estate. For just one house, there is the person who sells the house, the appraiser, the inspector, the mortgage broker or banker and the closer. And then maybe there is an interior designer, a painter, an electrician and a landscaper who are all involved in helping to fix up the house. There are developers who plan where new or renovated houses or commercial buildings will be built, finance people who run the numbers and marketing and advertising types who promote the project. And this is just one niche in the business world. Many of these jobs have required exams, but many have no degree or certification demands.

Another business niche that is growing is personal care. That includes things like hair care, manicurist, massage therapist, caregiver, etc. Few of these jobs, on average, meet the income threshold we have set for this book. However, individuals who do these jobs can make more than $20/hour. As an example of the range, the young woman at the local discount salon reports making between $10–$12/hour with tips, but the woman working in a high end salon who spent about $5,000 for a year of community college training says, "I started as an assistant at $10/hour. After a year, I was able to start working on my own. It took about two years before I hit $40,000/year and now, ten years from when I began, I earn $100,000 or more." Aestheticians can also see high earnings if they have good skills and marketing savvy. "No problem clearing $80,000 a year," says the woman who micro blades eyebrows and tattoos eyeliners. Fitness trainers and sports coaches have similar stories about a wide range in earnings.

Because there are so many different kinds of business opportunities, networking really pays off. Think about places you like to shop, products you care about, subjects that interest you. Talk to everyone you know – friends, family members, former teachers.

Since business is about making money and keeping track of that money, there is opportunity for those who like working with numbers. While management jobs will usually require a degree, you might get started with bookkeeping or inventory control work, learn on the job and work your way up.

Entry-level opportunities are everywhere and if you pay attention, show up and make yourself valuable, there may be ways to earn more or move into better jobs. Just walking around my little corner of the world, the young man who helped me at the bank had a story about how he switched from a low paying sales job to a job at Chase Bank and worked himself up to a middle management role. My accountant is looking for a part-time person to help for $15/hour with chances to grow. The gym across the street wants desk people part-time. The pay is only $12/hour, but you can learn enough to pass an exam to become a fitness instructor. At least five restaurants in the neighborhood have help wanted signs. A shop that refinishes brass and silver items says it's desperate to find people to train. These jobs to start don't meet our salary criteria but are all ways in to successful businesses with no up-front training.

The more you learn about a business, the more valuable you become and the more you will be worth to the employer.

See the note below for a description of the many careers in this field.[42]

So far, the discussion has focused on finding work in businesses that exist. Perhaps you want to consider starting your own small business. You will need to have an idea that you are convinced is in demand. Then you have to produce the product or service, win customers and deliver at a profit. Only about 20% of startup businesses get past the first year. Of those, half are gone by the end of five years.[43] So if you think you have a good chance of being one of the successes, hedge your bets. Get rid of debt. Find a way to live inexpensively. Be willing to put much of the rest of your life aside for a while.

42   https://www.realestateexpress.com/career-hub/real-estate-salary/30-real-estate-jobs-and-their-salaries/
43   https://www.usatoday.com/story/money/business/small-business-central/2017/05/21/what-percentage-of-businesses-fail-in-their-first-year/101260716/

Small businesses that want to reach their market now have a way to do that through e-bay and Amazon. In 2016, Amazon said half of its products came from small businesses and more than 100,000 businesses exceeded $100,000 in sales through the Amazon system. Amazon has begun a lending program to help those businesses grow.

Sometimes it's a good idea to start small and see what happens. A food cart is easier to start than a restaurant. Going to people's homes to cut their hair can be a step towards opening a salon. If you have sewing skills, you can make drapes or quilts or clothes from home. Plumbers, electricians, mechanics, painters and other tradespeople can become solo businesses, starting as one-person operations and, if it works, grow with more employees.

Whether you are planning to stay small or aim to go big, you will be wise to know how to identify and target your customer market, how to do basic accounting and produce a profit and loss statement and how to communicate successfully with your customers and colleagues. You can learn this from books, online information, mentors and just plain observation. I am struck by how often businesses don't return phone calls or fail to follow up on promises. While you may, in a particular week or month, be on overload, neglecting customers means that they won't be there when you need them again.

8. SALES/RETAIL

Sales is part of business but it is such a huge sector of the economy –involving over 14 million Americans – that it merits its own category.[44] It is a field with enormous opportunity, low barriers to entry and a wide salary range.

As an example, look at grocery stores which are everywhere and employ the largest number of Americans – over a million – working in sales. Many of the jobs are part-time and minimum wage, but there is also opportunity.

In San Diego, I met a college dropout who worked her way up from checker to an entry management position meeting our salary requirements in five years. She liked the benefits, the opportunities for training and the options for increased responsibility. Another woman, working in different national chain, didn't want management responsibility but loved that she could work just 30-hours/a week for full benefits, earn $21.15/hour (it took five years to get there) and feel her colleagues were family. However, she noted, the job kept her on her feet the full shift, it involved lifting and climbing to stock shelves, and the schedule had her working weekends and many holidays.

Sales people in her chain are hired for their ability to interact with customers. Grocery experience is not required, but good communication skills are mandatory. All store managers, who can earn $100,000 or more, are promoted from within. As with so many careers, you work your way up the ladder and prove your worth.

Think about places that have large numbers of employees with different job levels. For example, if you start working at Costco as a cashier or stocker, you are likely to earn between $10 and $14/hour, but if you work your way up to a supervisor you can earn over $40,000/year with benefits.

To move up, you must develop a reputation as reliable and hard working and be a person your colleagues respect and the customers like. You can learn these skills by watching how successful employees behave and asking for feedback from your supervisor.

---

44   https://www.bls.gov/oes/current/oes410000.htm

The least lucrative part of sales is retail sales associates who work in walk-in stores like those you might find at your local mall. Some stores offer commission opportunities so that if you sell more, you can earn more, but many jobs are hourly and there is no guarantee of hours. These jobs are declining as on-line buying increases.

More lucrative are non-retail sales. Here sales representatives sell goods and services to businesses, government agencies and other organizations rather than directly to consumers. Manufacturers and wholesalers rely heavily on sales reps – also called manufacturers' representatives or manufacturers' agents – to market merchandise, which might be anything from laboratory equipment to soft drinks. Two traits critical to succeeding as a sales rep: an enthusiastic personality and a tolerance for travel. Sales reps might also have administrative duties such as analyzing sales statistics and filing expense accounts. See the article in the note below for more information on a sales career.[45]

Yes, there is lots of stuff we can buy on-line with a click, but men and women are out in the work world every day selling construction supplies, utilities, agricultural products, telecommunications equipment, real estate, financial products, textbooks, advertising . . . and the list goes on. For example, Renee sells marketing and gift items to large profit and non-profit companies that then give them to their clients, and she helps customize the product. Joe sells security systems and works with buyers, often businesses, to fit the product to meet their needs. Samantha sells medical products to hospitals, and Ben sells social media consulting to entrepreneurs.

Check the employment opportunities website of every major firm in your area for sales openings.[46] The more you know about the product you are selling and about the needs of the customers who are buying, the more likely you are to be successful in sales. And it helps to have a tolerance for rejection and the ability to get along with a variety of people.

45   https://www.themuse.com/advice/how-commission-works-plus-everything-else-youve-ever-wanted-to-know-about-working-in-sales
46   https://blog.hubspot.com/sales/types-of-sales-jobs

9. MANUFACTURING

Manufacturing jobs are those that create new products, either directly from raw materials or from components. Usually this is done in a factory, plant or mill, and about 12.5 million Americans are working in these manufacturing jobs. In 2016, they earned $82,023 (includes pay and benefits) on average. That's 12 percent more than the average worker.[47]

Here are jobs that fit into the manufacturing sector:

- Assemblers and Fabricators
- Bakers
- Dental Laboratory Technicians
- Food Processing Occupations
- Jewelers and Precious Stone and Metal Workers
- Machinists and Tool and Die
- Medical Appliance Technicians
- Metal and Plastic Machine Workers
- Ophthalmic Laboratory Technicians
- Painting and Coating Workers
- Power Plant Operators
- Printing
- Quality Control
- Semiconductor Processors
- Sewers and Tailors
- Slaughterers and Meat Packers
- Stationary Engineers and Boiler Operators
- Upholsterers
- Water and Wastewater Treatment
- Welders, Cutters, Solderers
- Woodworkers

The Bureau of Labor Statistics describes what these jobs are like, how much education or training is needed, and the salary level. It also will tell you what it's like to work in the occupation, how many jobs there are, and whether it's a growing field. You can find our what particular skills are used, whether specific certification is required, and how to get the training needed by opening the note below.[48]

Manufacturers are always searching for more cost-effective ways of producing their goods, and that now involves using advanced technologies which are changing the skills requirements.

47   www.thebalance.com/manufacturing-jobs-examples-types-and-changes-3305941
48   www.bls.gov/ooh/production/home.htm

According to a recent report, 80 percent of manufacturers report a moderate or serious shortage of qualified applicants for skilled and highly skilled production positions.[49]

Over the next decade, nearly three and a half million manufacturing jobs will likely be needed, and two million are expected to go unfilled due to the skills gap. Other jobs that require less skill are being lost. Slowly apprenticeship programs are being designed to address the needs of advanced manufacturing.[50]

49   https://www2.deloitte.com/us/en/pages/manufacturing/articles/boiling-point-the-skills-gap-in-us-manufacturing.html

50   https://www.doleta.gov/oa/brochure/2007%20Advanced%20Manufacturing.pdf

10. INFORMATION TECHNOLOGY (IT)

This is an exploding field. "Jobs requiring computing and data science skills are likely to be the 21st-century equivalent of mid 20th-century factory jobs – the backbone of a prosperous middle class," wrote the former President of Yale University in the New York Times.

There is high demand now for jobs of varying complexity relating to information technology. All of those jobs do not require a college degree in computer science as explained in the article in the note below.[51]

For a time, coding was the hot ticket into technology, and there is still intense demand for highly skilled programmers who can program for AI, artificial intelligence, as well as general coders. Immersive coding bootcamps have sprung up over all over the country. These are usually short-term, for-profit enterprises that can work well for people without college degrees.

Just as we have to have auto mechanics to maintain cars, there is a growing need for people to maintain the machines and software that underpin the IT industry; yet there are not clearly developed educational pathways. Google is working to create courses that can provide this training[52] and believes that in eight to twelve months, people can lean enough to be effective in the workplace. AT&T is another example of a company investing in retraining workers. Registered apprenticeship programs are available in some locations.

There is increasing demand for medium-level digital skills. These jobs do not require coding or maintenance, but they ask for a fluency with computer programs and often, with social media. These, increasingly, are the skills now required for many administrative jobs in which technology is needed to distribute inventory, plan events, track donors, maintain scheduling. Administrative assistants with the skills to use technology to handle correspondence, travel and meeting arrangements and scheduling can, depending on location, meet the $20/hour salary criteria and exceed it.

51 https://www.themuse.com/advice/why-you-dont-need-a-4year-degree-to-get-the-tech-job-of-your-dreams
52 https://www.nbcnews.com/think/opinion/digital-technology-must-empower-next-generation-workers-not-alienate-them-ncna838806

11. TRANSPORTATION AND LOGISTICS

When our kids were little, they had a big picture book all about cars and trucks, boats and planes. All that movement was exciting, and they liked to zoom around the living room pretending they were going somewhere. The field of transportation lets you get into those diverse vehicles and go somewhere for real. If you click on the site in this note[53] you will find four pages of jobs in transportation with the median salary and education requirements.

The 3.5 million truck drivers in the US make up the largest segment of transportation jobs. On average they earn about $40,000/year, but the field is rapidly changing. There are concerns that self-driving vehicles will replace drivers. Perhaps there will be fewer positions for people to drive but new kinds of openings for people who can manage new kinds of vehicles.

Truck drivers need commercial licenses and schools that teach the necessary skills can cost several thousand dollars. Look for apprenticeship programs if this is a field that interests you.

There is such a wide range of careers in transportation. You can drive a taxi, a limo, a truck, a train, a plane or a forklift. You can be a conductor, a courier or a captain on a ship. There are jobs organizing shipping or repairing vehicles or managing inventories. Salaries are all over the place. You might begin earning less than $20,000/year but have the possibility of doubling and tripling that. For example, a beginning flight attendant can earn as little as $16,000/year. The median salary is about $37,000, and men and women with seniority at major airlines can top $40,000. Or work your way up to become a distribution manager and you can hit six figures. Take a look at all the options and think about whether there is something that seems right for you.

The latest major entry for jobs in transportation is on-demand drivers working for groups like Uber or Lyft. I have spoken with drivers in several cities who are earning more than $40,000 from this work, but all report that they must drive nearly every day, start work early and work into the night. Many more drivers

53   http://www.owlguru.com/career/list/transportation/

appear to be working on a part-time basis for supplemental income. To fairly assess income, you have to take in to account the increased costs of insurance, maintenance and fuel. And the presence of these drivers has seriously hurt the income of taxi and limo drivers.

12. ENERGY

The U.S. Department of Energy released a report in 2017 with a snapshot of what is happening with employment in the energy sector which employs nearly six and half million Americans. There are six components of this sector:

- the petroleum industry, including oil companies, petroleum refiners, fuel transport and end-user sales at gas stations
- the gas industry, including natural gas extraction, and coal gas manufacture, as well as distribution and sales
- the electrical power industry, including electricity generation, electric power distribution and sale
- the coal industry
- the nuclear power industry
- the renewable energy industry, comprising alternative energy and sustainable energy companies, including those involved in hydroelectric power, wind power, and solar power generation, and the manufacture, distribution and sale of alternative fuels.

About half the jobs are in traditional coal, oil[54] and gas production[55]. Jobs related to coal are declining[56], but opportunities for workers in natural gas, solar and wind are increasing. Less than half a million people now work in solar and wind but significant increases are projected.

There are many jobs in these areas that do not require education beyond high school, but work in renewable energies which include hydroelectric power, wind and solar power and other alternative fuels often demand advanced training or several years of related experience. For a long list of jobs in the energy sector and their requirements, click on this numbered note.[57] You can click around this site and find jobs in the industry by type and geographic location.

---

54   https://us.oilandgasjobsearch.com/
55   http://www.snelsonco.com/jobs-in-natural-gas-industry/
56   https://www.washingtonpost.com/news/wonk/wp/2017/03/31/8-surprisingly-small-industries-that-employ-more-people-than-coal/?utm_term=.b2229c7c6dd8
57   http://www.khake.com/page49.html

Look at this note for a description of six pathways for careers in the energy sector. Both apprenticeship and academic options are described.[58] Six high demand energy careers with apprenticeship options[59] are:

- Electrician, Powerhouse
- Gas utility worker
- Line maintenance
- Instrumentation Technician
- Refinery Operator
- Substation Operator

58   http://www.cewd.org/roadmap/
59   https://www.dol.gov/apprenticeship/industry/energy.htm

13. ARTISAN/ARTIST

Talent, persistence and, finally, a well-developed portfolio are the keys to a career in the arts. Whether you want to paint, make jewelry, design custom birdhouses or even custom coffins, create sculptures, design dresses, hats, boots or baby clothes or do anything else that involves making things by hand, you will have to prove you abilities just to get started.

People who chose this as a career almost always do so because they cannot imagine doing anything else and being happy. Producing something of meaning by hand feels deeply satisfying and feeding one's creative juices gives life a special zest. That's the very good part.

The more challenging part is that buying the work of artisans is a luxury for most people, and marketing is a constant challenge. This article by a photographer outlines the difficulties.[60] And this article offers strategies for working successfully.[61]

In spite of the difficulties of selling one's work, the median income for artists in this country is over $20/hour. That number averages the highest levels with the lowest, but it tells us it certainly possible to do well in the arts. Artists of all sorts are often able to maintain their primary artistic interest by combining it with a related activity like teaching or working in a business connected to their craft.[62]

Being successful depends more on talent and effort than educational background. The rewards of creativity need to be recognized, even if they are not always expressed in monetary terms. So if this is you, go for it. But keep developing your networking and marketing chops along the way, including social media skills, while attending to your craft.

60   https://www.huffingtonpost.com/hayleyroberts/twelve-things-no-one-tell_b_11538950.html
61   http://reddotblog.com/5-strategies-successful-artists-follow-to-thrive-in-their-careers/
62   https://www.bls.gov/oes/current/oes271013.htm

14. ENTREPRENEURSHIP AND FREELANCE WORK

Entrepreneurship, which crosses all sectors, has great opportunity and great risk. Instead of starting at the bottom, you start as CEO of you own business, which usually means that when you start out, you have to do everything on a shoestring.

There is some confusion about the difference between entrepreneurs and small business owners, which the article in this note explains.[63] About six percent of the U.S. adult population owns their own businesses. Some smaller percentage would qualify as entrepreneurs.

Entrepreneurship, according to Business News Daily, involves creating something out of nothing. Entrepreneurs are not people who believe in small. They are willing to take big risks for big rewards. To be an entrepreneur, you not only need to have an idea that you are convinced people will want, you need to convince investors to fund your start-up operations. To be successful, you will need eventually to provide a high level of return to your investors while many small businesses are satisfied with personal profits.

You must have passion, persistence and the ability to recruit and motivate a great team. The article in this note talks about what contributes to entrepreneurial success and failure.[64] A serial entrepreneur who started four Internet businesses remembers 18-hour workdays regularly and too many all-nighters. While you are working incredibly hard, there is usually no regular paycheck and no benefit package, but if you get it right, you can do very well.

An increasing number of people identify themselves not as entrepreneurs but as freelancers who work, often at home, on revolving projects. Freelancing is not about what you do but how you do it.[65] Freelancers are coding, editing, writing, fixing, cooking, coaching and more. Sometimes, they might join company teams and have contracts for a specified amount of time. Other times they might work in a consulting capacity or simply sign on for specific job. Some freelancers get

63   https://www.entrepreneur.com/article/233919
64   https://www.entrepreneur.com/article/288769
65   https://www.thebalance.com/what-is-freelancing-1794415

work through sites that aggregate freelance talent, and others develop jobs themselves – or both.

Today, more than a third of the US work force works as freelancers and by 2027 freelancers are projected to the majority of US workers. If you are good at what you do and go beyond doing the work to thinking about how to organize the work, you may find you have built a successful freelance practice for yourself.

5

WHEN/WHERE/ HOW TO DEVELOP NEEDED SKILLS

There are plenty of jobs that don't require any post secondary school. But most of them are not discussed here because they do not meet the career requirements we discussed earlier, especially the goal of reaching $20/hour. Certainly, these jobs may be the right starting place for now. Often, however, it takes targeted education to get to reach your career goal. More and more jobs are asking for certification or credentialing. Do not rule out these options because, in the past, you were not successful with school.

Perhaps you wanted college and couldn't afford it. Maybe you tried and it didn't make sense then. Maybe unexpected demands of life got in the way. Or maybe, school wasn't your thing and now, you are not sure you can grab hold again. But grabbing hold is just what it takes. Here is information about where and how you can do that.

▶ Learning How to Learn

Donald Rumsfeld was a former Secretary of Defense who made some big mistakes because of what he didn't know he didn't know. Here is what he says about knowing:

> There are known knowns. These are things we know that we know.

> There are known unknowns. That is to say, there are things that we know we don't know.

> But there are also unknown unknowns. There are things we don't know we don't know.

We can ask questions about what we know we don't know. The challenge is to figure out what we don't know that we don't know.

Maybe that includes a career choice that you never considered or ways to develop skills of which you were unaware. It might have to do with people who can help that you never imagined could be there for you.

Don't be afraid of what you don't know or of doing enough exploring to know more than you know now. Because of the Internet, it has never been easier to hunt for information. There is so much information, it's easy to feel overwhelmed. And then, once you get the information, you may still have to seek out people who can help you understand all the details.

If you don't know how to research online, an excellent place to start your education is finding out how to use the Internet for research. Here is a note about a free online course that will be useful now and, I promise, it will be useful later.[66] This could be the first new skill you learn.

If you find yourself struggling, do not assume you are inadequate. It can be difficult to figure out the right questions. It can be more difficult to get the right answers. I urge you to adopt this one rule: I DON'T GIVE UP.

Think of information as a jigsaw puzzle for which you have to collect the pieces. Keep pushing to figure out how to move forward. Ask for help. Go meet the people you think might have answers. Talk to others who have already walked the path that interests you. Find some cheerleaders who will give you encouragement.

Consider the Johnny Appleseed model. The story goes that Appleseed, an apple farmer actually named John Chapman, kept moving westward planting apples. According to the legend, he planted seeds by the bushel; some took hold and many didn't. I like that method – just keep hunting, looking, asking, planting seeds of your own until something sprouts.

▶ Two Stories

Many years ago, I interviewed a young man who had been a gifted and successful opera singer – until he was so unhappy with singing that he couldn't go on stage and had to walk away from a lucrative contract. He had no college degree, no skills other than singing. He went to work in a record shop and was starving. One day, walking to work, he saw an ad at Fidelity Financial for an entry-level job. He applied and was hired for not a whole lot more than the record shop. But the job offered benefits and continuous opportunity to take exams that allowed him to provide an increasing level of services. Eventually, he worked himself into a marketing job, and when I met him, was the head of marketing for a large Boston health organization. He described his transformation this way:

---

66   http://www.futurelearn.com/courses/searching-and-researching

I had been a star early on in music, and I was pretty arrogant. I had to learn humility and had to work really hard to learn all these financial things about which I was clueless, but every time I mastered something on my own, it felt so good, and it kept getting easier. Music always came easy to me. I liked that I had to work for this on my own. It gave me a kind of pride I didn't have with singing.

There is interesting research that tells us that the better we become at doing something, the more we like what we are doing. I interviewed a guy who had been through a bunch of jobs, fired from most, and was down on his luck. He landed a job as a customer service phone rep. . . . you know, the people we call to complain. When he started, he hated the job, hated working in a huge bullpen with dozens of other telephone answerers and with bosses looking over his shoulder. But he knew he didn't have many options, and he didn't want to live on the street, so he gritted his teeth and showed up every day and did whatever he needed to do to keep from being fired. And then, he decided he wanted a raise and he did a bit more. In time, but not right away, he earned the raise. Then he thought, "Well, what if I could become a supervisor?"

Here's what he told me:

I walked, emotionally, up hills and down valleys, I felt like I was waking on ice or through shit or in the desert. I wanted to give up lots of times, but I couldn't because I had to make this work. I didn't see any more choices for me. And after a while, I stopped being completely hardheaded and angry, and it stopped being so hard. And then I got good at it, and I started to like it. And then they made me a supervisor. And after that, I got another promotion. And I was a f*!**# failure at everything when I started, so if I could do it, just about anyone can do it.

▶ Embrace Force

Let's own up to the fact that making ourselves do things that seem difficult, that we are not sure how to do, that we would prefer to avoid is HARD, HARD, HARD! There is a TED Talk[67] online that speaks to just this. The speaker, Mel Robbins, tells us:

67   http://www.youtube.com/watch?v=Lp7E973zozc

Anything that is different from our routine requires FORCE. You are never going to feel like doing something difficult or uncomfortable. So get past your feelings. Stop waiting 'til you are in the mood. Just force yourself, right now. If you force yourself enough, you actually change your brain and it becomes less hard.

You don't need brains, money, magic or luck to make changes in your life. You need habit, unrelenting, no-you-can't-quit, just mark off thirty days, no excuses habit. This note takes you to a short piece that explains what it takes to change your life.[68]

If you have been out of school for a while and/or you never really felt like your best self in the classroom, you might want to start doing some foundation work on learning how to learn. Start with this quick seven-minute TED Talk about learning how to learn[69] and then you can follow up with a free online class.[70] It's a bit academic, but stick with it and you will find helpful information.

The most important skill for the future is your ability to learn new things. The world of work is changing so quickly that, no matter the category, you will be called on to figure out things that you may not imagine right now. This sounds a bit scary, but don't be afraid, be ready. Right now, this minute, is the time to start learning how to learn.

▶ Where to Learn

The title of this book promises information on jobs that don't require a college degree. What it doesn't promise because it would be a very foolish promise is well-paying jobs without having acquired good skills. Your charm, looks or quick patter, not even your desire to work hard, will be enough if you don't have the knowledge to do a job. Much of the time that means you are going to need more education. Your challenge is to figure out how to get the education you need to do whatever it is you want to do.

---

68   https://medium.com/the-mission/if-you-can-do-it-every-day-youll-be-enormously-successful-c264481d84e9
69   https://www.youtube.com/watch?v=O96fE1E-rf8
70   http://www.coursera.org/learn/learning-how-to-learn

I don't know you. How could I know you? And yet, I have confidence that nearly everyone who reads these words has the ability to learn. Some people have to go slower and spend more time at it, but if the drive and determination are there, odds are good that you can reach your goals IF you don't get scared, discouraged, depressed or diverted along the way. If you have people in your life who want to put you down and discourage you from learning, close your ears. Find better friends.

Sadly, your education may cost money. Sometimes, you will qualify for a grant or other kinds of tuition assistance, but often, you are on your own. Still, where is a better place to invest than in your future? See the section on p.69 for Help With College Tuition.

Certainly, formal education has value and is often the ticket for admission to a career. But lasting value is built on expertise, commitment, drive and the ability to get along with others. Focus unrelentingly on developing expertise in an area and commit to doing good work and being a person of integrity. If you can do that, the odds very much favor your success.

▶ School

The traditional way to get career credentials is to go to school. But what kind of school, what kind of credential? The credential choices are:

- Certificate – this attests to your having completed a curriculum that provides base level knowledge in a chosen field. Most frequently certification comes from an accredited school or apprenticeship program. The time it takes to earn a certificate varies by career. It can be several months or several years.

- License – this is issued by a governmental body and allows you to practice a particular profession. Usually passing an exam and/or demonstrating adequate experience are required to be granted a license. Sometimes, you must earn a certificate and then pass a state licensing exam.

- Credential – this is issued by a non-governmental body and validates by exam and/or experience a baseline level of competency. Often this comes from a national professional organization that has set practice standards for the field.

WHEN/WHERE/HOW TO DEVELOP NEEDED SKILLS   65

- Degree – this comes from completing an academic college program. People who satisfactorily complete the equivalent of two years of college work earn an Associate Degree, usually granted by a community college. Those who complete a full four-year program earn a Bachelor's degree. Additional work can lead to graduate or professional degrees.

When you are considering any program, you want to research:

- Cost
- Time
- Program options
- Graduation rates
- Employment rates
- Public reviews.

Don't make a quick choice based on what a buddy did or friend suggests without exploring all your options. This can be frustrating but go ahead, get a little frustrated if it means, in the end, you have better, clearer information.

I wish I could say, "Do this!" or "Don't do that!" Instead, I have to say, "Well, it depends. . ." What this section aims to do is explain your options so that you begin to have a sense of where you might look for information:

▶ Community Colleges

- Community Colleges offer two-year associate degrees that stand alone and can be used to transfer to a college granting a bachelor's degree. Most community colleges also offer academic readiness programs and certificate programs.

- Community college certificate programs are an excellent way to learn skills that are in demand and pay well. The note below provides a good article from the US Dept. of Labor about certificates.[71] (Also see Apprenticeships below.) Certificate programs range from a few months to two years depending on the profession. An ever-increasing number of careers require certification. For example, all the health care careers need this.

71   https://www.bls.gov/careeroutlook/2012/winter/art01.pdf

- Every community college does not offer the same menu and sometimes different branches of the same school offer different programs

- Community colleges charge by the credit hour. The credit hour cost varies among kinds of schools and by states, but, on average, figure between five and eight thousand dollars for two full-time semesters each year if you have residency in that state in addition to living and transportation expenses.[72]

- There are now some opportunties for free or reduced community college tuition. At the start of 2018, the city of San Francisco and the state of Tennessee offered free tution to in-state residents. Investigate the current options. Different cities and states also offer certain tuition advantages.

It should be simple to go online and find out all you need to know about certificate programs at schools near you. It is not. Nor is it easy to pick up the phone and call. Here is your best bet. Go online and type in the name of the school that interests you and the program and the words "information session" to see if there are regularly scheduled information sessions that will answer your questions. Then write down all the questions you have and take the list with you and make sure you get answers to all of them while you are there.

Some of the most popular programs, especially those in the medical field, can have wait lists and may require prerequisites and certain GPAs before you can apply. Enrollment is less difficult in many other certificate programs. Check all this out online and then in person. Think about whether you have family in other parts of your state or even other states (but you will have to earn residency status there to enroll at the lowest rates) where you can live if there is a program that will admit you more quickly or is better suited to your interests.

▶ Four-Year Colleges and Universities

While the focus of this book is on work that does not require a four-year degree, if you are re-thinking your education strategy, don't ignore the bachelor's degree option. If you had decent high school grades and/or have good college admissions test scores, this is worth exploring.

---

72   Tuitions do vary. You can shop around, but for the best rates, unless you win a scholarship, you must be live in the state in which the school is and there is usually a year's residency requirement to be considered an in-state resident.

In this note is a list of 100 most affordable small colleges in America. Some are public schools that favor in-state residents but many are private.[73] A private college will not necessarily cost you more than a public college since you do not have to be an in-state resident, and you will not pay by the credit hour.

▶ Trade Schools

- These are private, profit-making institutions organized to prepare students for a specific trade. There is a great deal of controversy about trade schools. Some have been accused of offering poor preparation, luring students into financial aid packages they don't understand and may not be able to pay back and even closing without warning.

- Private trade schools are usually more expensive than other options, but they can require less time to graduate and may have fewer requirements to enroll.

- Trade schools can be the choice best suited to you. It's just that it can be hard to tell the good from the bad. See the article noted below for some advice about how to decide.[74] Because trade schools are businesses, they are more focused on selling their services than suggesting alternative paths for you.

▶ What About Online Learning?

You can find online education programs at any of the kinds of schools described above. You can earn a four-year undergraduate degree almost entirely online, doing your schoolwork from the kitchen in your pajamas. The great thing about working online is that you can usually work whenever, wherever it fits your circumstances. But you miss out on developing relationships with your teachers and your classmates.

Many students report that they do much better when they show up for classes. Teachers have a harder time figuring out just what you might need online. Fellow classmates are less likely to offer support and suggestions. The lively interaction that can come from real-time discussion is lost. It can be lonely to work online

73   https://www.bestvalueschools.com/most-affordable-small-colleges-america-2015/
74   https://www.consumer.ftc.gov/articles/0241-choosing-vocational-school

and harder to feel encouraged and motivated. If you are just starting out, consider trying to do in-person classes initially, and then decide what is best for you. If you must work online only, try to develop personal relationships in whatever ways your course suggests. At the least, find one other person you can meet with periodically to review the class material.

▶ About Learning

Researchers find that more education, on average, leads to a higher salary, but there are plenty of exceptions. I'm pretty sure my car mechanic out-earns me. And in the last decade, in some states, community college graduates were out-earning four-year college grads.[75] Many young people with college degrees who do not have useful skills and the ability to connect in the work world are finding themselves unemployed or underemployed. But this is not an argument against education. It is an argument in favor of planning your education to get where you want to go – oh, and about having some idea where that might be.

Don't let this information discredit a four-year college education. If you commit to learning all you can in college – or anywhere else–, there is the opportunity for great wisdom and personal growth. As we said at the start of this book, if you want stuff, you need to be able to earn the money to pay for it. But having stuff is only one part of a good life. Learning to appreciate art, books, diversity, curiosity, research, science – all sorts of things that a good education can provide – makes you rich in different ways.

Learning how to learn is your most valuable of skills. Simply going to college doesn't make that happen. You have to engage in the experience and want to find the juiciness in it. The goal here is not for you to have a degree; it is for you to find ways of working that bring you both satisfaction and sufficient resources and to develop the ability to keep learning all through your life.

Whether you go to school full-time or part-time, do whatever it takes to pass your courses so you are not paying for a class you must repeat. Ask for tutoring, go to all extra sessions, set up a study group, get a mentor, do the homework twice.

75   *Job U*, Nicolas Wyman, p. 52

Practice "deep work." Deep work means that you shut out everything that is unrelated to your primary goal. Don't allow distractions. No Facebook posts, no cell phone chatter, no video games. Yes, sometimes a break helps to keep your focus, but the best breaks are often exercise or walking quietly or listening to music for ten minutes but not engaging in distractions that are likely to keep you from returning to your work. Work hard for 90 minutes; take a ten-minute break or a 30-minute exercise stint and then back to work. Do that for three or four times a day when you can.

Or set up a rigid schedule. Get up at 5 A.M. and work for two hours before you allow the rest of your life to intrude. Or set aside focused time at the end of every day. This is very hard when you are just beginning. Force yourself, and, in time, it becomes easier and easier to do.

▶ Help With Tuition

Are you single without kids? Consider spending a couple of years earning as much money as you can while taking a few classes to keep your learning skills up. Don't buy a good car with a car note, don't spend much money eating out, don't smoke – it's expensive. So is alcohol. Live at home if possible. Don't engage in unprotected sex that could result in an unexpected child. Save money to finance your education, and then spend it to prepare for a better life.

If you have family responsibilities, apply the same thinking. Perhaps one of you can work while your partner goes to school, and then you can trade. Be patient. You can have a jazzy car, restaurant meals and nice clothes, but postpone that until you have the skills you need for good work and a good income. The road is long . . . no need to rush down it.

Explore scholarships and state programs designed to help you with your education. Every state is different with different eligibility criteria. On the CareerOneStop website from the Department of Labor,[76] you can find the nearest American Job Center. Click the *Find Local Help* button towards the top of the site, type in your zip code, and it will tell you the closest center. They may be able to direct you to financial aid related to your getting back to school.

76 www.careeronestop.org

Depending on family income, you may qualify for grants and/or loans. Both private and public, non-profit and for-profit schools offer financial aid. Income is a key factor, but there are also merit scholarships based on ability and talents. Make sure you understand the interest charges and the repayment schedules on any loans. Be very careful – even reputable schools have left students saddled with big loans and few job prospects. And with for-profit institutions, their first purpose is to make money, not necessarily to give you the best possible counseling.

In the numbered note is an article that describes the different kinds of funding generally available.[77] Specifics change so check for the most current information, and absolutely, make an appointment with the financial aid counselors at whatever schools interest you. But verify whatever advice they give you. It's a good idea to put what you understand in writing and ask the program director to date and sign it for you.

A few states have begun to offer students help with tuition not covered by grants and scholarships. Read the noted article to see if anything can work for you and then look for updated information.[78] There is a trend starting for states to consider making community college tuition free although there are usually income and residency restrictions.

One way to deal with tuition is to get a job and go to school while you are working and try to pay for as much as you can without loans. This is slower; sometimes it makes sense to push through, go to school for a couple of years full-time, and get a better paying job as soon as you can – but not always. The plan that you can make work is a good plan.

Some companies, like Starbucks, offer employees help with tuition. See this note for information on other companies.[79] It may make sense to earn less in salary and get tuition assistance. Another way to get help with tuition is to spend a year doing national service with Americorps or Vista.[80] Sadly, the future of these programs is unsure, so always check and see what is possible when you are ready.

77   www.schoolguides.com/The_Most_Common_Sources_of_Financial_Aid.html
78   http://money.cnn.com/2017/05/16/pf/college/states-tuition-free-college/index.html
79   https://www.cnbc.com/2017/08/23/these-companies-pay-for-college-tuition.html
80   https://www.nationalservice.gov/programs/americorps/americorpsvista

If you should end up continuing your education and graduating with a four degree, there is another option for tuition assitance. If you work full time after graduation at an eligible nonprofit or government agency while making steady student loan payments for ten years (120 monthly payments), and the federal government will forgive the balance of your student loans. Careers include teaching, social work, military service, disability assistance, emergency management, and others. However, the political situation may end this option or change the rules so again, check very carefully.[81]

If you are not sure you can handle the demands of school, start slowly and let yourself grow into it. If you starting at 25 or 30 or beyond and worry that you are getting old, remember that you are going to be older with or without education. Better with! You can, perhaps, work towards one year's worth of courses on a part-time basis and then go full-time for your second year. Noted is a list of the best schools for adult learners.[82] Read about options for work and learning here.[83]

If you have a criminal conviction, federal money may not be available to you. Read about options for work and learning here.[84] The federal government also sponsors the federal "bonding" program, which may be able to help those with a record of arrest or conviction get a stable job. It's like an insurance policy on the employee, making it more attractive for a company to hire such an individual.[85]

▶ Apprenticeship Programs

In an apprenticeship program you earn and learn at the same time, and you begin immediately working in the field that interests you. This is an excellent option for people who want to learn more skills but need to keep working and avoid debt.

■ Apprenticeship programs can be sponsored by one employer, multiple employers, or an entire industry (e.g., an association representing the industry). Unions also sponsor apprenticeship programs as do educational institutions.

81   https://www.nationalservice.gov/resources/ed-award/loan-forgiveness
82   https://washingtonmonthly.com/magazine/septemberoctober-2016/americas-best-colleges-for-adult-learners/
83   https://careerwise.minnstate.edu/education/training.html
84   https://www.careeronestop.org/ResourcesFor/WorkerCriminalConviction/worker-with-a-criminal-conviction.aspx
85   http://bonds4jobs.com/about-us

Most states and many unions have websites that discuss apprenticeship programs for that state or trade. Type *apprenticeships* and the name of the state and/or trade in which you interested in your browser. Washington State, for one example, has a good site. Check out their site for information that can be applied more generally.[86]

The United Unions is one of the many groups working to encourage apprenticeships. Here is a quote the UA site about construction apprenticeships:

> UA apprentices learn through both classroom and on-the-job training in what is considered by many to be the best construction industry apprentice program in the world. The five-year apprenticeship period is divided into one-year segments, each of which includes on-the-job training and related classroom instruction. All UA apprentices receive a strong general education background in the trade, with core courses in basics such as mathematics, mechanical drafting, and related science. At an appropriate juncture, apprentices can choose a specific curriculum to pursue with the goal of becoming a plumber, pipefitter, sprinkler fitter, or service technician in the air conditioning/refrigeration field, or any of the other many service opportunities in the industry.[87]

■ Apprenticeships in the trades are the most numerous for now, but lots of work is going on to provide apprenticeships in other job categories as well. There are apprenticeships in health care, advanced manufacturing, and transportation and logistics as well as other fields, but these programs are not available everywhere. One way to find out about apprenticeship programs is to go to an online site called My Next Move.[88]

There are lots of ways to use this site. For example, on the home page, look at the center box that says Browse Careers by Industry. Scroll down until you find a sector that interests you. When you click on that, all sorts of jobs will appear in a list. Again, click on one, and it will take you to a page with eight boxes that give you different kinds of information. Move down to page to the box labeled education. In that box are three buttons labeled *"find training,"* *"find certification,"* *"find apprenticeships."* Click on all of them.

---

86 lni.wa.gov/TradesLicensing/Apprenticeship/Become/default.asp
87 http://www.ua.org/apprenticeship
88 https://www.mynextmove.org/

Or go to the apprenticeship finder on the same My Next Move site. Type in the job that interests you and a city or zip code and apprenticeships will come up. All the places listed may not have training opportunities when you are looking, but check out all of them. Bigger cities offer more opportunities. Spend a couple of hours hunting and clicking and thinking about what appeals to you. You might want to think about moving to a city where you can find apprenticeship opportunities if there are not any where you are living.

- All apprenticeships that are registered with the U.S. Department of Labor or a recognized state organization have both on-the-job learning and classroom learning. The first focuses on the practical, hands-on skills related to the specific job. The classroom instruction focuses on the principles and theories that support what you are learning on-the-job.

  Apprenticeships in the trades are usually four to six years in length, but remember, you are working and earning the whole time. Other programs can be as short as a year or two. All the registered apprenticeship programs offer a Certificate of Completion. This certificate is recognized anywhere in the country, and it gives you academic credits on which to build if you decide to continue your academic education.

- Many companies with apprenticeship programs, but not all, pay for the classroom-training component; most unions also pay for the classroom-training component of union programs. In some cases, apprentices agree to stay with the program sponsor for a certain minimum amount of time or the apprentice must pay back the cost of the classroom component if they leave before the minimum timeframe. Compare salaries for both non-union and union programs as well as the costs that come with each program.

A recruiter for the plumbing union Local 68 in Houston, TX, Chato Woodard, arranged for me to go through their apprenticeship application process as if I were an aspiring union plumber. I want to tell you about the experience, but remember, different states, different unions, different companies, different schools–they all have different processes. Still, I think it's worth summarizing what I learned from my Houston union experience.

1. First, there was lot of paperwork for this union program. Don't panic. You can take as long as you want to complete it. Don't make my mistake. I was so eager to begin filling in the blanks that I didn't listen carefully to all the instructions and so missed hearing some details.

2. Second, I was surprised, as were others, that there was a twenty-question math test. The test required us to add, subtract, multiply and divide fractions. I couldn't remember exactly the method for multiplying and dividing. Just a small amount of time brushing up ahead of time will make this no sweat for you. Put "learning about fractions" in your browser, as I did when I got home, and you will get lot of sites. The one I liked best is mathisfun.com. There is no pass or fail score for the test, but getting a high score will help you in the selection process. I only scored a 70% – not so good. If I were serious about wanting to be a union plumber, I would follow the instructor's advice and come back for a re-take. "If you come back and re-take the test and do better, it tells us you are really serious about wanting to do this." Different trades will have different screening exams.

3. Read the online instructions for what you need to bring. In my case it was a photo ID, my social security card, my birth certificate and my school transcript. Check to see what you need, make a list on the front of an envelope and check things off as you put the papers inside. Here is something to remember: if you can't put your hands on your birth certificate or school transcript and diploma, you can write away and order them, but this stuff takes time, sometimes weeks, so absolutely plan ahead. There are some annual costs for an apprentice program, but you will be earning money to afford to cover the training costs and union dues if you are in a union program. Ask what these are upfront.

4. If you are naturalized citizen, you will need other documents. If you have a felony conviction, at least for this program, you need to complete the Texas supplemental criminal history form. (Other states will have their own requirements. Check out this note.[89])

5. If I were fortunate enough to secure an apprenticeship with Local 68, the union would place me in a job for the five years of the program and the first hour of pay starts at $19.13/hour. I will receive OSHA 30, the most intense safety training, in my first year. I will pay union dues, but I will be part of a pension program and have no cost health insurance. And if I am, someday laid off, I'll be automatically enrolled for unemployment benefits. In turn, I promise to work full-time for five years and take training classes either two

89   www.careeronestop.org/ResourcesFor/WorkerCriminalConviction/worker-with-a-criminal-conviction.aspx

nights a week or on Saturdays which equals 246 classroom hours/year. I will be subject to random drug testing and must adhere to the sexual harassment policy. The program is assigned an annual cost that I will pay off through work each year. If I leave the program without good reason, it is possible I will be asked to pay back the $2,000/year cost of my training.

6. With so many benefits, it is not surprising that that the demand is greater than the supply. In a recent selection round, 400 men and women applied and only 80 could be accepted. Women and vets are encouraged to apply. The minimum requirement is age 17 with a GED or high school diploma but recently, in Houston, between 25 and 30% had college degrees. The recruiter's advice: Show grit. Don't let a table of interviewers who don't look like you intimidate you. Keep applying – don't quit.

7. I was offered a few more bits of advice for his program: "Come to the union meetings. . . Eat the cookies and listen, then network. . . When you come for your interview – and everybody gets an interview – wear slacks and a nice shirt. . . . Don't chew gum; no ball caps in the building. . . . Relax and you will do better. One of the applicants in my group of people waiting to be interviewed says he had bought *Job Interviews for Dummies* and found it helpful.

And while it isn't supposed to work this way, who you know can help. Look for people working in the place where you want to work who might help you learn the best way to apply.

Check out this article noted below which was written for people interested in being an apprentice electrician; the advice is good for other areas as well.[90] And another article from the *Huffington Post* offers you useful background on community college apprenticeship programs.[91]

If you have been laid off or meet certain low-income requirements, you may qualify for supportive services that help you become job ready. There are 600 local boards (Workforce Development Boards) that have been established around the country to help with job training, both apprenticeships and other work options.

90   https://www.electricianapprenticehq.com/how-to-join-ibew-apprenticeship/
91   https://www.huffingtonpost.com/tom-snyder/apprenticeship-programs-at-community-colleges_b_8918366.html

Go to the CareerOneStop website[92] and look for the Employer Networks Finder. Click on it and type in your zip code and it will show you resources in your community where you can find employment support, including apprenticeship options.

▶ Jobs Corps[93]

This is a program sponsored by the U.S. Department of Labor for 16–24 year olds but the target population is 16–18 year olds who have left school. Applicants must meet the low-income requirements and need skills development. Job Corps offers residential living, meals, health care, training and a modest allowance. It can provide a childcare stipend as well for students who must cover childcare costs while in the program.

There are 119 centers around the country, and programs generally run from eight to 24 months.

Reports found online suggest the program places about 75% of graduates, but we could not find information about the kinds of placements or the salary. This program may be of special interest to those who feel they lack other educational options. It is difficult to figure out the details of the program on the program website. Find a Job Corps center near you and visit to get more information. [94]

There is a related program that is not part of Job Corps but may be helpful for young people ages 14–21. In some recent legislation called the Workforce Innovation and Opportunity Act (WIOA or "we-OH-uh"), new funding was set aside for eligible youth who are either in-school (14–21) or out-of-school (16–24). WIOA emphasizes services to out-of-school youth by requiring 75% of the youth funding a Local Board gets to be spent on these young adults. You can find out where your local board that administers these funds is by going to the note below.[95]

92   www.careeronestop.org
93   https://en.wikipedia.org/wiki/Job_Corps
94   https://www.jobcorps.gov/live
95   https://www.servicelocator.org/program_search.asp?prgcat=1&officeType_1=0boards.
     aspx?location=77019&radius=25&post=y&sortcolumns=DISTANCE&sortdirections=ASC&
     currentpage=1&pagesize=10&persist=true

▶ Military

For many men and women, the military has been their gateway to esteem, education and adventure. For others, it has been an unhappy commitment. And once you join, it is a commitment. You don't get to change your mind. So if you are thinking about this as an option, do the research and figure out just what you are signing on to do. Here is an excellent article, in many parts, updated in 2016, that gives you a comprehensive view of your options and what you can expect. Get a cold drink or a hot coffee, find a comfortable chair and read all the segments for an excellent overview of what it means to consider the military, including pay levels and benefits.[96] Another helpful article talks about ten things you should know before you join the military.[97]

If you hunt around on the Internet, you will find lots of different viewpoints. Before you commit to several years of your life, commit to several hours to get a handle on whether this is for you. Talk to people who love being part of the U.S. military – there are thousands – and talk to those who felt it was not a good choice for them. The military can be a path to educational opportunities after discharge, and it can be a career option. Initially, the pay is low for enlisted men and women, but in time, you can earn the $40,000/year amount this book has as a parameter. Here is an article that summarizes pay.[98] It is undated so the figures may have increased. Figure out who you are and what makes sense for you.

Just one caution: don't choose the military for negative reasons. For example, don't sign up because you don't know what else to do or you don't like school or you can't bear living at home anymore. The military offers tremendous opportunities for personal development and skills building if you are open to what is presented for you. "You can, at a young age, have more authority, more responsibility, more significant work in the military than anywhere else I know," one advocate enthused. In speaking with military men and women, it is impressive to hear how proud they are to serve their country and make meaningful contributions, but, as they stressed, you have to be ready to set aside your own wishes and commit to follow the orders you receive from your commanders.

96   https://www.thebalance.com/what-the-recruiter-never-told-you-3332706
97   https://www.military.com/join-armed-forces/top-10-things-you-should-know-before-you-join-the-military.html
98   https://work.chron.com/much-enlisted-army-soldiers-make-28798.html

You will be able to select what kind of career direction you want, but each pathway comes with a specified military obligation. Generally, three-year contracts offer the most limited training options. If you receive more sophisticated training, you will be asked to commit to a longer period of service. And, in times of crisis, your training expectations can be overruled by the needs of your officers.

Many men and women are attracted to the military for educational benefits. The benefits are excellent, but they vary depending on the length of service. Unlike earlier benefits, today's education benefits don't expire and can be used in a variety of educational settings including apprenticeships (and depending on your work in the military, you might even be eligible for apprenticeship credits) after you leave the military. Read up first in these two articles so you know for what you will be eligible.[99] [100]

You will also be eligible for education benefits even while you serve. You can use up to $4500/year for tuition assistance for online or other classes while you enlisted.

Recruiters can answer your questions, but their job is to sell men and women on joining, and they are encouraged to meet signing quotas so talk to people who have gone before you to get their points of view since once you sign on, you are there for your term of service. Ask for written explanations if you feel confused. And then put your own understanding in writing and send it back to your recruiter. Don't hesitate to ask as many questions as many times as you need to ask until you are clear about your commitment and your benefits.

In the past, one attraction of the military has been the retirement system. This has changed in recent years, and you want to be sure you understand the rules. Find this out in the article in this note.[101] Also, be aware that when you retire is not entirely up to you. The military may decide it no longer needs your services and you will not be able to re-enlist even if you wish although the head of the San Diego Military Advisory Council says that those men and women who are successful in their jobs and show a commitment to their service are rarely separated against their will.

 99   https://militarybenefits.info/forever-gi-bill/
100   https://www.military.com/education/money-for-school/education-benefits-in-the-military.html
101   https://www.thebalance.com/understanding-military-retirement-pay-3332633

▶ Alternatives to School

Some people just can't sit in class. Others aren't able to follow a regular school schedule. Some don't yet have the confidence and discipline to hang in there and do the schoolwork. And some feel the costs are too high. It isn't always necessary to pay other people to help you learn skills. But you do have to exercise internal motivation and self-discipline.

If you feel committed to a purpose for yourself, that motivation and discipline are possible even if you are busy with work and family. Cut back on TV or the Internet or being distracted by nothing much. Commit to finding 20–30 minutes every day to educate yourself. Make the effort here, and it is likely to make it easier to make an effort elsewhere.

My friend Ben earns $70,000 a year working in a computer technology startup. He did not learn his skills at his highly ranked private university or the expensive law school that left him dissatisfied. Rather, his office was in a space that also housed a coding camp. When coding classes were over each day, Ben would stop his work and have a coffee with the coding students and ask about what they learned. He read the textbooks they were assigned, figured out who were the best of the group and sought out their help. He became an expert coder for free but the cost of coffees and his own efforts.

It isn't that college doesn't matter. Often employers want a college degree as an entry requirement because it seems to say something about intellect and focus. But thousands of jobs are going unfilled because employers can't find people with the skills to do the job. Focus on the skills, and remember, they are not all technical. Knowing how to communicate effectively, how to control your temper, how to listen well – all the things we discussed in Chapter 2 are also important skills.

What follows are some alternatives that can help you learn on your own. Maybe they will get you ready for more formal schooling or maybe you will just become more skilled by your own independent efforts.

Before you follow this route, you might want to invest in an unusual book that talks about how to be an effective learner. *The 5 Elements of Effective Thinking* by Edward B. Burger and Michael Starbird is $12.75 on Amazon and one of the best books I have ever read about how to learn. Read it and then read it again. You can certainly get it through your local library, and it comes in an audio version. Another powerful book for leaning how to learn is *A Mind for Numbers: How to Excel at Math and Science (Even If You Flunked Algebra)* by Barbara Oakley. (And it's helpful for more than math and science.)

- **Watch TED TALKS**. Ted Talks are short presentations by experts designed to be presented to people who are not experts. They are generally 18 minutes long. There are thousands of them. You can watch them on your phone anywhere, anytime. Here is the entire list of talks.[102] Just pick out what interests you.

  There is a tremendous amount of learning to be had here at no cost. You just pay with your attention. You might want to keep a small notebook and write down things that really mean something for you.

- **Take free online classes through MOOC, Mass Open Online Courses.**[103] These are college level classes taught by college faculty from around the world in more subjects than I can list. They are all free. You just pick what you want and sign up. If you don't want to receive a $49 certificate of completion – and you probably don't – there is no cost. If you find the class is not right for you, you can stop without any penalty. Of course, that's the hard part. Since no one is watching you and there is no price for stopping, it's easy to decide you are too busy and quit. Start out by promising you will take one entire course all the way through. Then you can decide if you want to take another. To make it easier to find the courses you want and the best ones currently offered, this site has sorted through the courses and organized them for you by category.[104]

  One of the groups that provide MOOC courses is called Coursera and they are just now in the process of designing learning paths to help people figure out what sequences of courses make sense for various career goals. Check it out here.[105] MOOC options that allow you to earn certified transferable credits are now growing. You can't earn a degree for free, but this can help you can manage both debt and time commitments. See the noted article.[106]

102   www.ted.com/talks
103   MOOC.org
104   https://medium.freecodecamp.org/200-universities-just-launched-560-free-online-courses-
      heres-the-full-list-d9dd13600b04
105   blog.coursera.org/new-coursera-start-finish-learning-paths-starting-new-career/
106   https://www.class-central.com/report/moocs-for-credit/#moocs-for-credit

■ There are **thousands of YouTube videos waiting to teach you everything** from how to fix your disposal to how to put on eyeliner. Just Google something you want to learn and find a video. They are usually straightforward and short and you can watch as many times as you need to until you understand. A guy I know just avoided a $500 auto dealer bill by using YouTube to figure out how to take off the car door panel and install a new side-view mirror he ordered for $160. His degree is in economics, not engineering, but he knows how to read and to watch videos. "Ended up taking me only thirty minutes, and it wasn't so hard."

A really great online resource is **Khan Academy**. For free, on your own schedule, you can tutor yourself in math, science, art history, grammar, history, computer programming, computer science and economics. Khan is especially strong in teaching math. Lessons are broken down into small bites. Once you figure out where you need to start, you can go forward step by step, repeating each section as many times as necessary until you own it.

Another resource is **Skillshare.com**.[107] People with passion in an area post online classes here. Anyone can post a class so you will want to check out the reviews to find those that work best. There are thousands of them and many are free. This is an excellent place to learn about particular skills that interest you.

■ **Read.** Maybe there is something you want to learn for which there is no book yet written, but, truly, there isn't much that hasn't been written about. You can go to Amazon.com, type in a subject and see what books are there for the buying or go to a bookstore. But for free, get yourself to your local library, take proof of residency (it can be a local utility bill) and get yourself a library card. Then the librarian can help you find books about whatever captures your curiosity. Doesn't matter if your library doesn't have the book you need; it can be ordered for you at no cost. So can videos. And beyond whole books, there are magazines full of articles about specific topics: *Popular Mechanics* for repairs, *National Geographic* for exploration, any number of do-it-yourself repair books and instruction manuals. Just ask and odds are, you will find.

You can give yourself a free college education just by reading. You might not get a degree, but you will end up knowing a lot. Related to reading, build your vocabulary. Learn a new word every day and find a way to use it in conversation. This website gives you ten other websites where you can learn a word a day in different ways.[108] One great way to learn new words and new facts as well is to do crossword puzzles. The *USA Today* site will give you a new puzzle every day.[109]

If you want to get started learning new words right now, load this app on your iPhone, and it will send you a word every day.[110]

- **On The Job Training**. Use your work place as a school. Sign up for whatever learning opportunities you can. Let your supervisors know you are eager to learn more and ask if they can help you. Ask your coworkers if they can teach you skills. Sometimes people won't help because they fear you are competition and sometimes employers have no interest in helping you grow, but if there are ways to learn at work, take them.

- **Home Projects.** Pick a project and just figure out how to do it. It might be to build a shed or fix an old car, make a table or sew a dress. Start muddling your way forward with books, videos, questions to friends and even strangers. Maybe the first results won't be terrific but you will be learning with both success and mistakes. My friend Carlos never got beyond the 8th grade, but he finally got up the courage to leave his job in a shipping department and start his own home repair business because he has taught himself plumbing, painting, electricity, carpentry, flooring and more.

Or find a buddy who likes to share his or her interests and see about working on a project together so you can learn. Be willing to let the other person be in charge. Once you have new skills, you can do it your way. Don't worry about failure. Failure is a step in the direction of getting better. People who never fail are often the people who never try.

The overall point is Do Something. The more you learn, the easier it is to learn more. The world of work – indeed, the world of life – is changing at ever-faster speeds, and that means where we are now might not be where we need to be in a decade. So go get some learning chops. You could get hooked.

---

108   www.makeuseof.com/tag/10-websites-learn-word-day-enrich-vocabulary/
109   http://puzzles.usatoday.com/
110   https://itunes.apple.com/us/app/word-of-the-day-daily-English-dictionary-app/id987136347
       ?mt=8

6

HOW TO LOOK
FOR JOBS

▶ 24 Tips On What Will Help You Find Good Work

1. Start at a low level if that's what needs to happen, and build up skills and experience. Maybe you are only making minimum wage to start but after a year, you can say you have a year of experience in the field and that can qualify you to apply for better jobs. The grocery store cashier now making over $40,000 started out at minimum wage.

2. Educate yourself about the field that attracts you. Read books, watch videos, do online research. Be able to talk intelligently about what you want to do. The more you understand about a field and its options, the better positioned you are to find what works for you. If you seek out people doing work that interests you and are able to ask interesting and thoughtful questions, you will make a positive impression. That's how my exterminator hired his assistant.

3. Take classes. Do something/do anything to give you some basic knowledge of the field and demonstrate that you are seriously interested. If you are working and have a family and little flexible time, find something online. Or try the local community college. Or take a continuing education class that you find.

    You can use evidence of your classwork to show your serious interest in a career, and perhaps the teacher will become a reference or resource. A young woman I coached loves fitness and has an undergraduate degree in health education. But it was earning her training certificate, online, from the American Exercise Council that opened up her ideal jobs.

4. Hunt around online for organizations that address the field in which you are interested. Join if you can. Many have dues that may be an obstacle, but check it out. Go to meetings if they meet near you. At first, you won't know anyone and will feel odd, but keep at it. Talk to people. Ask questions. Listen to the speakers and read any publications the organization produces. Volunteer to do things to help the organization. Working on a committee is a great way to develop relationships with people in a field that interests you, and this can lead to a job.

5. Find a magazine, journal or newspaper that talks about the field in which you are interested. Subscribe. Read regularly. For example, *Referee Magazine* is about $47 for a year's subscription and free if you read it in the library. It provides all the latest information on regulations applying to pre-collegiate

sports. Are there blogs written by people active in the your field of interest? If you were interested in *Referee Magazine,* maybe you want to check out the blog soccerrefereeusa.com. See if you can find online posts about work that interests you and read them regularly. Sometimes, job leads may surface in your reading.

6. Get to know people who do what you want to do. Ask all your friends and people where you worship and/or work, ask your relatives and your neighbors for the names and contact information of people doing what you hope to do. Contact them and ask for half an hour of time to have them tell you about the field. If they don't return your call, don't take it personally. Just try again with someone else. If you do make contact, try to maintain a relationship with the person over time if it feels right. Write to thank them for their time if they do meet with you.

   More jobs are found through personal contacts than online posts. If you want to build guitars or lead mountain treks, exercise horses or manage bingo games, you are not so likely to find job leads posted as passed on from people already doing the work.[111]

7. Be outstanding at what you are doing now so that you merit great recommendations and people who know your work say good things about you. Excellence is rare, and it attracts attention.

8. Volunteer if possible for something related to what interests you. In this way, you will get knowledge, meet contacts and see opportunities when they arise. Or just volunteer in the community. Often in volunteer roles, you meet people from all around the community, and you don't know who might be the source of a good lead.

   Maybe you want to be a volunteer firefighter, help out at the local health fair or work the pumpkin patch at your church. Drive the coffee cart at the local hospital, get involved with community theater, help with the local marathon or spend some afternoons as a Big Brother of Big Sister. Many communities have volunteer centers that help match volunteers with organizations. The local United Way might be a source of ideas.

111   https://www.salary.com/11-odd-jobs-with-high-salaries/

9. Apply, apply, apply. Often you apply for a job and never hear a thing. Keep applying. If it's possible, ask for feedback on why your application did not merit even an interview. Get some expert advice on your resume as you apply. Ask people you think can give you good advice to look at your resume and applications. Look at a helpful resource for writing a good resume.[112]

10. Look for job announcements everywhere and anywhere. Look at all the job postings sites, and every time you see a job that sounds interesting to you, apply. Don't procrastinate. Apply quickly. Looking at postings will help you understand what employers want and what they may require.

11. Take all the educational opportunities your current job offers. One of my rules of thumb is that nothing turns out to be irrelevant. Even if you think a course is not directly useful to you but it is offered to you, especially if it is offered at no cost to you, maybe you should just take it.

12. Develop your communication skills. If you are uncomfortable speaking or writing or working with a computer, finds ways to practice and become better at these skills and more comfortable practicing them. Many jobs, especially those that involve dealing with the public, value your ability to talk well with others as much or more than having specific work experience.

13. It is not always possible, but sometimes, the boldest and most effective strategy is to stop what you are doing and take yourself back to school full time to get a certificate or associate degree in what interests you. Maybe you can keep working and go to school nights. Online is increasingly an option, but it's good to have interaction with others who are interested in what interests you. Down the line, these people could be the source of jobs or potential hires for you. Or maybe you can find an apprenticeship and work and learn at the same time.

14. Have a vision. If you don't know what you are looking for, it might come right past you and you will never notice. I have been struck by how needing to know something suddenly brings information or people related to what I want to know to my attention. When I tell people what I am looking for, I get the benefit of their networks as well as mine, but I can't tell them if I don't know what it is.

112   https://www.myperfectresume.com/resume-templates

15. Become computer literate. If you are already skilled at typing, using aps on your phone and finding things on your computer, good for you. If you are not, start working on this. Computers are more and more a part of work across all sectors, and your comfort with using them is an important skill no matter what you hope to do. You won't use online websites if you feel awkward on the computer.

16. Use online job search sites. Post your profile on the sites that allow it and set yourself up for automatic notifications of jobs related to your interests. At the end of this section is a list of online job sites you can use.

17. Identify a company that is new to your area or is growing and needs staff quickly. Apply for whatever job you can get and learn and grow on the job.

18. Be curious. Everyday, you are exposed to all kinds of work opportunities. This week, just by asking, I found out that the woman who checks out my groceries earns over $40,000/year. The guys who came to pump out our sewer line easily earn that. The incredibly capable Hispanic immigrant who came to help with a yard problem has started his own business and tops our income requirements. And the guys working on the street crew installing pipe also have solid careers.

    Most interesting, every one of these people likes what they do and is proud of their work. Talk to everybody about his or her work and see what you can learn. The young woman next to me at a bluegrass concert told me about a great job that pays well in the beverage industry. No college needed, and only three people had applied. Most people like to be asked about what they do. So ask!

19. Tell everyone you know – family, friends, people at church or on your basketball team – what kind of job you are looking for and ask them for help in finding it. Lots of people will just forget, but you never know when someone hears of a good job and thinks of you.

20. Go to job fairs, resume in hand. Dress well. Know what you are looking for and reach out to as many recruiters as you can.

21. Consider moving. If you find yourself in a place where there are not many job opportunities, you might want to consider a move. Perhaps you live in

a place where the cost of living is so high that you might do better with less salary and lower expenses. Just remember that often we have more flexibility than we realize. Sometimes, circumstances keep us rooted, but if you needn't stay where you are, decide if that's what you really want. But a caution: moving is expensive. You have start-up costs, you need to re-create a support network and you might not find a job quickly.

22. Look well groomed. Research tells us that people form a strong opinion of a prospective employee coming for an interview before that person gets from the door to the chair. You don't need expensive clothes but you want to look neat and clean. You want your appearance to say, "I'm serious about this job and interested in your hiring me." While it is much more accepted to be casual now than in previous decades, making an effort to "dress up" usually has a positive effect.

23. Put together a resume you can use on paper or post online. This is a summary of your schooling and your experience. If both are thin, you will have to figure out how to highlight your skills and your work ethic. Go online and read about resume writing. Remember one basic rule: don't lie. If you feel you have very little to put down under education and experience, maybe you begin with a summary statement that presents your best self. You might say something like "I am a formerly clueless high school graduate who has discovered both the pleasure and possibility of hard work and determination. I bring a commitment to hard work and serious learning and a desire to grow." If you have some good skills, you can use the brief summary to highlight them.

24. Be woke! If you don't expect anything from life, you increase the odds that life will not deliver much. Want more. Want to find work that brings you satisfaction and self-respect as well as a decent wage. You want to be in charge of you because no one else cares as much about you and your life as you do. Your parent or partner can't lead your life for you. You have to do it on your own.

▶ Where Can You Find Jobs?[113]

More and more, jobs are being posted online, not in the local newspaper. And more and more, applicants are asked to apply online. While many of the jobs you will find online ask for specific experience and/or a degree, you should keep looking with the hope of finding something for you– and keep applying.

Research has found that men tend to apply for a job if they have 60% of what is asked for. Women wait until they can meet all or most of the requirements. If you can't match the job profile at all, you are probably wasting your time, but if there is something that feels just right for you, apply. And then follow up with a call if you can figure out where to call or with email – unless it specifically says no phone calls.

It can be discouraging to apply online to job after job and have no response. So don't just rely on online options. Keep working your networks and looking for face-to-face opportunities to sell yourself.

Right now, as 2018 begins, the labor market is tight and it's a good time to be job hunting. Maybe down the line, things will change, but people get hired every day. Figure out ways to keep your spirits up and to keep going.

Online applications make it easy for people to apply so the pool of competitors is often larger than if you can find something locally and apply directly. Some employers don't want to bother sorting through a large stack of applicants and won't post. Sometimes, they ask current employees to recommend new hires, which is one more reason to let people know you are hunting.

If nothing is working, then maybe it is time to change what you are doing. You might have to get more education, start at lower level than you wish and develop better skills. But there is ALWAYS a need for men and women who work hard, accept responsibility, act with integrity, behave honestly and treat others with dignity. If that's you, please don't give up. The work world truly needs you.

---

113 The website www.thebalance.com was very helpful in identifying online websites. The main focus on thebalance.com is to provide financial advice most especially for millenniasl. It is full of good content and I recommend you check it out.

1. Look at company websites. Most large companies, national organizations and public bodies have websites on which they list career openings. Think about places that interest you and go looking online. You can apply online but you may also want to see if they will let you apply in person. For example, Costco will let you look at jobs by state and type.

2. Read the local papers. Sometimes, companies looking for people in a specific area will put ads in the local paper.

3. Read bulletin boards. Look for signs in windows or on trucks asking for help,

4. If there is a job that interests you, go to the workplace and ask if you can apply. If they say they are not hiring now, ask if they keep resumes on file or if there is a time when it makes sense to come back.

5. If you have a buddy with a job that interests you, ask him or her if it would be easy to make an introduction to a person with hiring responsibility.

6. Check out the online websites. Many of them, in addition to job postings, have advice about resume writing, job interviews and the job search process. These are not all the sites on the Internet but they are the most familiar and popular.

   - LinkedUp.com has millions of jobs which they have collected from job posts on company websites and which you can access by title and location. All kinds of jobs will show up here.

   - A related site is LinkedIn.com which is a job networking site where you can post your profile and skills and people interested in those skills can search. People who know and like your work can recognize you on the site. It's also a place where you can find others who are doing what interests you and reach out to them for information. There may be a cost to connecting with those people through LinkedIn.

   - Indeed.com claims it is a major website for job postings. It hunts for postings from other websites, but employers can also post directly at no cost. You can enroll to be notified of job postings in geographic areas of interest to you

   - CareerBuilder.com is another national site with a variety of listings.

- Dice.com is a site specifically oriented to tech jobs.

- Glassdoor.com provides job listings but also information gathered from employees about how much they like working for a specific company and about salary levels. If you are interested in a particular company, you may be able to find reviews from people who work there.

- Idealist.com is a good place to look for jobs in the not-for-profit world. It also has many volunteer postings so if you want to increase your experience while working in an area while doing something else, this might be a good way for you acquire those new skills or establish your reputation for good work.

- Monster.com is another large national job website that collects postings and aggregates them.

- Google for jobs was just unleashed in late 2017. Like other sites, it looks web wide for job openings. It allows you to target a specific job title in a specific place and will hunt on other job sites (but not Indeed.com) and send you the results. It also provides salary information. Google docs, which is separate, is one place to find a template for writing your resume.

- USAJobs.com is the official website for U.S. government jobs. If you're interested in federal employment, go there and develop a resume using the on-line tools available. You can develop more than one and call each something different. Maybe one resume works for a specific type of federal job but another resume works for a different type. Have the resume(s) ready for when a federal job opens that you're interested in. Then follow the on-line application process.

- Coolworks.com focuses on jobs related to the outdoors including camps and resorts. Many of the jobs here are seasonal and/or part time and would be excellent opportunities to develop skills and a work history. This site also has volunteer opportunities that provide living accommodations.

- Flexjobs.com is a site for people who want to work from home. It is not free. You can sign up for one month for $14.95 (with a refund option) or three months for 29.95. It seems to have good reviews online but there may be compensation for writing those reviews.

- Salesjobs.com focuses on sales related jobs.

- Healthcarejobs.com focuses on jobs in the healthcare sector.

- Craigslist.com is a localized online site for buying, selling and notifying. It has jobs that you can access by geography. It tends to have more free-lance positions and posts from very small businesses than other sites. With all sites, you should be cautious and check out employers, but this advice applies especially to Craigslist postings.

- In addition to these major job sites, there are scores of niche sites focused on particular sectors. This footnote takes you to a list of 100 such sites.[114]

▶ Remaining Optimistic

Job-hunting is work, tough work. It can involve lots of rejection or, maybe worse, lots of nothing. You send out applications and resumes and nothing at all comes back. It is easy to start taking this personally. "I suck," or "The world sucks." Rejection feels personal, but it is more structural than personal.

There is a system in place, and the system can't really tell from a one or two-page resume if you are a great person or not. It guesses and it tilts towards making the safest kinds of guesses. So if someone else looks better on paper than you do, you fall lower on the list. And the system is not designed to take a risk, to say, "I see something in this person, and I'm betting he/she is a winner even without experience."

What can you do? First, be realistic. Recognize that job hunting, especially when you have little experience or few credentials, is slow and challenging. Recognize that looking for work is, itself, work. But also recognize that part of what you need to do is to stay positive and determined.

That's a tall order. Here are some things that seem to help:

- Exercise. If you belong to a gym, GO. If not, go out for a morning and afternoon walk, go on a run, shoot some hoops, build a fort with your kids, ride your bike. If you can't go out, figure out an exercise routine to do at home. Moving

114   https://good.co/blog/list-of-100-niche-job-boards/

your body turns out to be very helpful for keeping your mind in a positive place and keeping your energy up.

■ <u>Have a routine</u>. When no one is counting on you, it's easy to stay up too late, get up too late, hang around, play some video games, and find you have spent a whole day doing mostly nothing. Instead, get up at the same time every day and get to bed at a decent hour for you. Set a schedule that establishes when you will exercise, when you will go online and look for jobs and when you will do other related activities. Most of us cannot spend eight hours applying for jobs, but we can block out periods of the day when we will focus intensely on our job search and then spend other time in related activities. Be your own boss and give yourself a work schedule.

■ Set targets for yourself. Maybe you will apply to a certain number of jobs every day, spend an hour exercising, reach out to two or three people for networking and read for an hour.

■ <u>Volunteer</u>. One way to keep from getting depressed is to do good things for others. If your only work is looking for work, make a volunteer commitment. It can be for one or two days a week, maybe only a few hours, but get out of the house and go do something that contributes to the well being of others. This really helps to feel good about oneself. If you don't know what to do, check out Google volunteer opportunities in your community online. Call the local hospital and ask what you could do or the Salvation Army or the Goodwill. Check with your local house of worship. Look on the Idealist.com website.

■ <u>Avoid negative people</u>. Sometimes there are people in our lives who are of no help at all. They insult us, tell us we are not worthy, remind us of past failures. These people are bad for our health and bad for our job search. As much as possible, avoid them and when you can't, do not pay attention. If you have friends who riff on how awful life is, get new friends. Attitude is critical to finding success, and you want to work hard at keeping a positive attitude.

■ <u>Look at alternatives</u>. If you keep trying and trying and can't get to where you want to go, maybe you need to go somewhere else for the time being. Suppose you have set your heart on a $20/hour job and it refuses to appear. Maybe for the short term, you have to work for $12/hour while taking steps that can get you to that better job. Or consider a job in an area that has opportunity, even if it doesn't seem to be your first choice.

- <u>Learn something</u>. You have time on your hands. Don't waste it. Do things that help you learn more. Chapter 4 has all sorts of ideas for how you can learn on your own. Watch a Ted Talk every day. Learn how to change the oil in your car or how to build a birdhouse. Decide you will make your first cake or draw your first picture. Keep your brain clicking. You might not yet be able to feel good about landing a job, but you can feel great about that cake.

- <u>Find a support group</u>. I can't tell you where to find people in your same circumstance, but I can pretty much promise you that there are people out there struggling in ways similar to you. If you can find them through a community group or job search organization, it can be a big help. Job-hunting can feel very lonely even if you are far from alone.

- <u>Find a career coach</u>. You might not be able to afford to hire a career coach but there may be people in your life who will do this at no cost. Find someone with whom you can check in every week that can coach and encourage you and give you more ideas. Being accountable to someone else helps us stay on track.

- <u>Have a positive affirmation</u>. Pick a mantra for yourself, something you can repeat whenever you feel discouraged. It can be spiritual: "I know a higher power will look after me." It can be energizing: "No slacking or sleeping. Game's just begun. Not over 'til I've won," It can be playful: "Hip hop, damned if I'll stop. I ain't no slob. I'll find that job." Find your own words and keep repeating them.

- <u>Don't give up</u>. I knew a woman who lost a $120,000/year job. She lost her house. She moved to be near her kids and lost her friends. She felt like she had lost her whole life, and it took her two and half years to land a new job. It paid $110,000/year and, in time, she rebuilt her life. She was as bright, hardworking and skilled when she had the job as when she lost the job and as when she got the next job. Who she really was didn't change but the circumstances of her world and then of her life changed. It was very hard to keep going. Please, keep going.

A CLOSING NOTE

I have been mentoring, coaching, teaching people for over 50 years. It is deeply satisfying to have a hand in helping someone grow into his or her fullest capacity. If this book can help you, it will be a great joy for me. I know one-on-one advising or coaching works better than a book, but I'm hoping a good book is better than nothing.

Here is what I can do to make this a bit more personal. If you have a question and want to email me, I will try to answer it. Send it to http://susanlieberman. com/work/question. If, suddenly, this invitation results in a deluge of questions, maybe I'm not going to be able to manage. But let's try.

If it doesn't work, I'll shut down the site and you will get an error message, but as long as I can do it, it will be fun to communicate with readers and know what you are thinking. Comments and questions welcome. And let me know if you find mistakes. I have tried so hard to make sure this book is accurate, but like you, I'm human. S.A.L.

ACKNOWLEDGEMENTS

I could not have written this book without all the conversations, both formal and informal, that men and women all over the country had with me. Sometimes, I met in an office and sometimes on an airplane, a supermarket aisle, an Uber ride. And most people were so kind, so candid, so willing to tell their stories and offer up what they had learned. To all those who helped in this way, my gratitude.

Many people read bits and pieces of drafts along the way or clarified data. But I want to single out just a few people who were so gracious in reading drafts and giving such productive comments. Maria Brady, Julia Garza, Mary McCoy, Bonnie Thomas, Trilla Pando, Paul Sanchez and Chato Woodard were exceptionally generous. Paula McColl and Karl Hunt helped with design issues when I really needed help. My son, Jonathan, is ever-patient with my computer questions and challenges.

All the young men and women I have mentored over three decades are woven into these pages. It was they who helped me appreciate how hard it can be to plot a future with little experience and insufficient guidance.

And, as always, my husband Michael sustains me in ways large and small, not the least of which is bringing laughter into our lives.